Mouse

Georgie Carroll

REAKTION BOOKS

To Felix, and all the mice that you were too dear,
and in the end too slow, to catch.

Published by
REAKTION BOOKS LTD
33 Great Sutton Street
London EC1V 0DX, UK
www.reaktionbooks.co.uk

First published 2015
Copyright © Georgie Carroll 2015

Printed and bound in China by 1010 Printing International Ltd

A catalogue record for this book is available from the British Library

ISBN 978 1 78023 339 0

Contents

Introduction: *Ridiculus Mus*

Parturient montes, nascetur ridiculus mus.
Horace, *Ars poetica*

The Indo-European word for mouse, *mus*, also means 'thief'. In Sanskrit, its diminutive, *mushká*, can be translated as both 'little mouse' and 'testicle'. Much of the etymology of the word 'mouse' has to do with an extraordinary relationship to fertility and destruction. In Latin *mus* or 'mouse' is connected to the word for 'fly', *musca*, and to other abundant parasites as diverse as *mush*rooms (taken from the word for 'moss', *mus'cus*). In his classic *Etymologies* of AD *c.* 615, Isidore of Seville teaches us that the mouse is also related to fertile soil, *humus*, because of an ancient belief that mice, appearing as if out of nowhere, were born directly of the earth.[1] It is perhaps only by coincidence that in some early Afro-Asiatic languages the word *mus* can mean 'penis', 'to give birth' or 'to be pregnant'.

In his book *Bible Animals* (1869), the English natural historian J. G. Wood describes the mouse as 'one of the most destructive animals in the world'.[2] In Hebrew the mouse is called *ackbar*, meaning 'destruction of the corn', and in Arabic *far ah*, 'corn-eater'. The Persian Magi, the wise men of the Gospel of Matthew, loathed the mouse, and granted any man who killed one the honour of having slain four lions.[3] The mouse's capacity to create and destroy is disproportionate to its small size. In fact nothing about the mouse is small, except for its relative proportions. Spatially mice defy scale. The rodents have colonized six out of

Anonymous
Indian artist,
*Ganesha with
Two Attendants,*
c. 1790–1825,
opaque water-
colour and
gold on paper.

seven of the world's continents, adapting to some of the harshest
environments on the planet, where few other land mammals can
survive. Mice are universally recognized as the most tenacious
of animals, thriving in spite of their countless predators.

In myth and medicine the mouse is traditionally regarded
as a sort of miracle maker, capable of seemingly impossible
feats. For their power, mice in antiquity were held sacred, forming the basis of an ancient cult that grew out of Egypt into Asia
and the Americas. Even today the mouse is the totem animal
of two of the world's most pervading household deities: the
Hindu elephant-headed Ganesha, and the Buddhist god of
wealth, Daikoku. (Of course Mickey Mouse has become a
sort of globalized postmodern totem, overtaking it would seem
the bald eagle as the symbol of the most powerful nation in
the world.)

Page 65

House mouse

Edward Adrian
Wilson, '*Mus
musculus*, House
Mouse', c. 1890–
1910, from a
collection of
pencil sketches
and watercolour
drawings of
British mammals.

Yet the mouse both defies its size and is defined by it. Mice are some of the world's smallest mammals. In myth the mouse is almost always the smallest character; the ultimate prey and therefore at the bottom of the natural, and cosmic, orders. Because of its size and vulnerability the mouse is often equated with that which is inferior, weak and pathetic; even the banal and the unexotic. In Slovenian 'a mouse's penis' is the smallest thing imaginable.

In the English language 'mouse' can refer to a shy, timid and quiet person, and to be mousy is to be dull, nervous and lacking in presence or charisma. We ask a person who shows a lack of strength whether they are a man or a mouse. In a proverb attributed to the Roman poet Horace (65–8 BC), the mouse symbolizes ultimate disappointment following a boastful promise, when a 'mountain labours and brings forth a ridiculous mouse' (*parturient montes, nascetur ridiculus mus*).[4]

The *Oxford English Dictionary* defines the mouse as a small rodent with a pointed snout, relatively large ears and eyes, and a long tail. In general use, the word 'mouse' can refer to any small mammal, such as a shrew or vole. Historically 'mouse' was a much more obscure term, categorizing a great number of rodential species. The oldest book of zoology, the Babylonian Harra of *c.* 2000 BC, which lists a number of Akkadian and Sumerian animal epithets, highlights early attempts to categorize rodents – to include species of hamster, gerbil, rat, mole-rat, shrew and vole as well as mice – under the appellation 'mouse'.

Perhaps because of the animal's familiarity, the mouse's name is commonly lent to other animals. 'Mouse' is used as a prefix or suffix for a plethora of different mammals, birds, insects and invertebrates in order to signal certain attributes or behaviour (mouse-deer, mousebird, mousemoth, mousespider, seamouse). Apparently even molluscs can appear like mice. The mussel, imagined as a sort of 'mouse of the sea', takes its name from the Latin *musculus*, meaning 'little mouse', owing to its shape, colour and abundance. In the Dutch language a *mus* is a sparrow, the commonest of birds.

Yet despite its supposed familiarity, most of us are more at home with the mouse's artificial guises than with the mouse itself. We are much better acquainted with fictional mice and with images of mutant laboratory strains. Even an Internet search for 'mouse' brings up a computer mouse before a real one. Most of what we do know about the mouse's biology and behaviour comes from research using the 'lab mouse'. Although the mouse has more to do with our domestic space than any other wild mammal, it remains largely a mystery, inhabiting secret spaces within our homes that we cannot see: inaccessible labyrinths between walls and under floorboards, accessed only through the mousehole, a door to another world. When we do see a mouse, the experience is almost always short-lived; the darting ball of fur and flash of tail that appears and disappears before we have a chance to notice it: to appreciate the colours in its pelage, the smoothness and length of its tail, the shape of its nose, its delicate whiskers and tiny claws.

Writing a book about the mouse may seem something of a *ridiculus mus* in itself; sometimes requiring justification, it would seem, for why a 'worthier' animal had not been chosen. The mouse is not generally deemed majestic or beautiful, characterized by a naked, primordial tail. And yet it seems that the world has a unique, albeit resentful, affection for the mouse. The minutiae of the natural world, mice remind us both of nature's power and of our own humble place within it – 'the best laid schemes o' Mice an' Men'. As Robert Burns wrote of this 'wee, tim'rous beastie', this 'fellow mortal', the mouse represents the very foundations of the natural world and of human society, and all that is fragile and vulnerable to 'man's dominion'.

Mouse explores this rodent in its many forms, whether brave, resilient, powerful or adaptive; worshipped, mutated, slaughtered, loved, loathed or feared.

1 The Evolution of the Mouse, from Prehistory to the Laboratory

Although the house mouse (*Mus musculus*) is defined by human space, it lived for millions of years before mouse and hominid were ever properly acquainted. To the mouse, its ancestors and the prehistoric mouse-like mammals that lived alongside the dinosaurs, humans have played a very small part in a 250-million-year history. Like hundreds of other mouse species, many house mice, despite their names, live distinctly from human habitations, where they are integral to delicate ecosystems. House mice have even been introduced to and thrive on many sub-Antarctic islands uninhabited by human populations. The house mouse is called vermin because it lives on what others have provided, like a parasite, from the Latin *vermis* or 'worm'. Yet humans have been convenient rather than necessary hosts to the house mouse over the past million years or so, as man the gatherer became man the farmer,[1] providing the mouse with surplus food, shelter and protection from predators to some degree. Human exploration, trade and agriculture have since aided the house mouse in becoming the second most widely distributed mammal on earth after the brown rat (*Rattus rattus*).

Following humans closely in their pursuits, the house mouse has constantly been implicated in human modernity. The animal's radiation across the globe maps out the history of our own movements as well as our economic history, and its more recent guise

Anonymous, Japanese drawing of a mouse from the Edo Period (1603–1867), ink and sepia on paper.

A house mouse assesses the situation from a gap in a woodpile.

of lab mouse continues to reflect stages in Western scientific development. Even the hyperreal computer mouse is a sign of our technological advance.

In this way the mouse has become a symbol of and tool in our progress; a sign of our sophistication as a species. And yet, an animal of unsurpassed evolutionary success, it is also a reminder of our own fragility. It could be that this apparently insignificant creature, having lived for millions of years before us, will live for millions of years after us. Echoing mythic visions of the apocalypse, scientists predict that ultimately mice and rats will inherit the earth. The idea is the stuff of satire, a vision of the world turned on its head. Douglas Adams acknowledges the ironic potential of our oldest adversaries in *The Hitchhiker's Guide to the Galaxy* (1985), in which the giant computer that is Earth is governed by hyper-intelligent mice. Warner Brothers introduced us in the animated children's television series *Pinky and the Brain* (1995–8) to a megalomaniac laboratory mouse, 'The Brain', who every night, with the help or hindrance of his simple sidekick, tries to take over the world.

What we know about the house mouse's behaviour and biology derives almost entirely from studies on mice in *our* world: from generations of mice genetically engineered in sanitized, industrial laboratories; mice that lead entirely different lives from the wild mice that we will never know under our floorboards or on remote islands.

'Mouseness' has existed on earth for around 250 million years. It is a model that works. The mouse is one of the most successful, fastest-evolving animals on earth; a relative of one of the 2,000

Green-glowing mice used for studies in DNA, born green all over including almost all of their organs and cells.

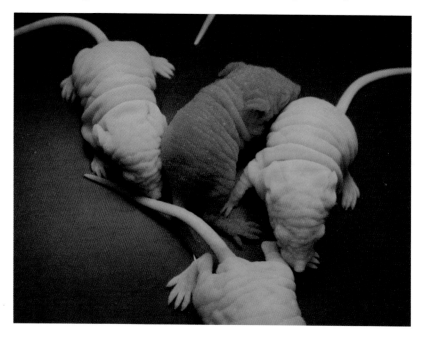

Impressions of 'mouse-like' rodents: the chinchilla and the spiny pocket rat. From an edition of the Comte de Buffon, *Compléments du Buffon: Races Humains et Mammifères* (1838).

species of rodent that account for over half of all living mammals. Mice reproduce at some of the lowest and highest temperatures of any mammal, which explains how they are able to flourish in some of the harshest polar, dry and tropical climates on earth. It seems that the anatomy and survival mechanisms of mice as we know them are relatively unchanged from those of the prehistoric 'rodents' that marked the beginning of mammalian evolution. These animals' small size, ability to burrow, omnivorous diets, rapid rate of reproduction and adaptability to environmental change allowed them to survive the mass extinction event that wiped out 85 per cent of life on earth 65 million years ago (MYA).

One of the earliest mouse- or shrew-like mammals is the *Megazostrodon* of the Triassic period (250–200 MYA), a small, hair-covered animal with a long, naked tail. Its name, meaning 'large girdle tooth', from the Greek *mega* (large), *zostros* (girdle) and *odon* (tooth), refers to the large external ridges of the upper molars. Unlike modern shrews, mice or rats, *Megazostrodon* laid eggs, with placental development appearing later in evolution. The subsequent Jurassic period (200–145.5 MYA) marked the evolution of the most diverse and long-lasting order in natural history, the Multituberculata, known as the 'rodents of the Mesozoic'.[2] The Multituberculata, also identified by their dental anatomy, are named after the cusps or tubercles in their teeth. Like Rodentia, the order comprised burrowing and arboreal species ranging in size from a very small mouse to a beaver. Following the extinction event, Multituberculata became widespread and diverse in the northern hemisphere, quickly diversifying and diverging into thousands of species that were now able to grow and colonize the Earth in the absence of dinosaurs. Thought to have been herbivorous, they thrived during the emergence and radiation of flowering plants from the Cretaceous period (142–65 MYA) through to the Eocene epoch (54.8–33.7 MYA), when they were replaced by 'true rodents'. It is thought that some species of 'true mice' originated in Asia sometime during the Paleocene epoch (60–55 MYA), which means that mice derive from an ancestor that may precede us by as much as 50 million years. One of the oldest known rodent fossils is that of *Ischyromys*, a giant two-foot-long mouse-like true rodent from the early Eocene. This tree-dwelling rodent is held to be an ancestor of the modern dormouse family Gliridae. By the end of the Oligocene epoch (33.7–23.8 MYA), a period of cooling when grasslands began to expand, making way for fast-running

prey and predators, over half of all living families of rodent had appeared.[3] The increased aridity in the subsequent Miocene epoch (23.8–5.3 MYA) and the emergence of deserts in the Pliocene epoch (5.3–2.6 MYA) made way for the evolution of mice that characteristically hop or jump, animals that form the superfamily Dipodidae, such as jerboas in the Old World and pocket mice, so named because they store food in the pockets of their cheeks, in the New.[4]

A great number of Old World rats and mice, if not all, are thought to have diverged from a common squirrel-like ancestor, *Progonomys*, between 14 and 8 million years ago. The order Rodentia, under which both species are categorized, takes its name from the Latin *rodere*, meaning 'to gnaw'. This characteristic trait – which can be blamed for the ill-fated and even demonic reputations of mice and rats on account of the damage it causes – is designed to keep short constantly growing incisors, which allow the consumption of foods that are inaccessible to other animals, such as nuts and wood. Mice and rats were not properly distinguished from one another by name until *Rattus*, suggested as a subcategory by the German naturalist Fischer von Waldheim in 1803, became popularly used for rats in the late nineteenth century.[5] Earlier naturalists, including Linnaeus (1707–1773), had used *Mus* to describe both species collectively.[6] In 1855 the German naturalist Johann Friedrich von Brandt categorized rodents as being mouse-like (Myomorpha), porcupine-like (Hystricomorpha) or squirrel-like (Sciuromorpha).[7] Approximately two-thirds of rodents are constituted by species of mouse and rat, along with other myomorphic species such as hamsters, lemmings and voles. Most myomorphs, including the house mouse – but with the exception of dormice (Gliroidea), kangaroo and pocket rats and mice (Geomyoidea), and jumping mice and jerboas (Dipodidea) – belong to the largest living rodential group and complex superfamily, Muroidea, under which six families, nineteen subfamilies, around 280 genera and at least 1,300 species are classified.

The superfamily Muroidea is largely divided into the first and second largest mammalian families, the Muridae and the Cricetidae, which represent what are known as Old and New World rats and mice respectively. The Muridae, to which the house mouse belongs, is the larger of the two families, and includes more than 700 species of true mice and rats. The true ancestor of Muridae is still unknown; however, the rodents are thought to have originated and diversified with the spread of grasslands in Asia in the Early Miocene epoch (23.8–5.3 MYA). The earliest molars currently accepted as murine belong to *Antemus chinjiensis* from 13.75 million years ago in the Siwalik Hills of northern Pakistan. The Muridae became common around the world during early human migration, when the glaciers began to retreat during the Holocene epoch (*c.* 11,500 years ago), and are now distributed throughout the entire western hemisphere. The Cricetidae have been equally successful, occupying most of the world: all of Eurasia, all of the western hemisphere and East Africa. Old World rats and mice represent over 500 of the 700 species of Muridae, forming a subfamily, of which the house mouse is also a member, known as Murinae, a hugely diverse group that has radiated rapidly in Europe, Africa, Asia and Australia. The Murinae are in fact the only terrestrial mammals to have reached Australia without human agency, crossing when sea levels were low some 4 million years ago.[8]

Within the Murinae family is the genus *Mus*, meaning 'mouse'. All members of the *Mus* genus are referred to as 'mice', although the word 'mouse' can refer to species outside the genus, or even outside the superfamily Muroidea. *Mus* or 'murid' lines

Barbary striped grass mouse (*Lemniscomys barbarus*).

Mus Darwinii.

emerged by the early Pleistocene epoch, approximately 2.5 million years ago, with a number of species in Eurasia, eastern Africa and possibly one or two island communities.[9] However, *M. auctor*, considered the earliest fossil of *Mus*, is thought to have derived from *Progonomys* 5.7 million years ago.[10] Murine archaeology is acknowledged as a complex area of study on account of the fact that the bones of burrowing animals are neither easy to date, nor to tell apart from those of other rodents.

Today typical subgenera of *Mus* exist in East Asia (*Coelomys, Promys*), Sub-Saharan Africa (*Nannomys*) and Eurasia and North Africa (*Mus*). *Mus*, the subgenus, which is referred to by the same name as the genus to which it belongs, includes a number of species,

An illustration of Darwin's leaf-eared mouse (*Phyllotis Darwini*, formerly *Mus darwinii*) from coastal central Chile (1839).

An anonymous
19th-century print
of mouser cats.

such as the Algerian mouse (*M. spretus*), Cook's mouse (*M. cooki*), Cypriot mouse (*M. cypriacus*), fawn-coloured mouse (*M. cervicolor*), earth-coloured mouse (*M. terricolor*), house mouse (*M. musculus*), little Indian field mouse (*M. booduga*), Macedonian mouse (*M. macedonicus*), *M. nitidulus*, Ryuku mouse (*M. caroli*), servant mouse (*M. famulus*), sheath-tailed mouse (*M. frailicauda*) and steppe mouse (*M. spicilegus*). The house mouse (*M. musculus*), so named by Pliny, meaning 'mouse little mouse', is now distributed worldwide.

The house mouse has four largely accepted subspecies, which include *M. musculus castaneus* of South and Southeast Asia; *M. m. domesticus* of Western Europe, North Africa and the Middle East, and later, via exploration and colonization, of Australasia, the Americas and sub-Antarctic islands; *M. m. musculus* of North and Central Asia, Eastern Europe and Scandinavia; and *M. m. bactrianus* of Central Asia and Afghanistan. The short-tailed *M. m. musculus* travelled to Britain through Russia and Central Asia, while the long-tailed *M. m. domesticus* extended through North

22

Africa and eventually into Spain. The length of the tail is typically an indicator of climate, with longer tails developing in warmer regions and shorter tails in colder ones. *M. m. domesticus* reached Britain via Iberia, but is not thought to have arrived until the late Iron Age, when it followed farming routes and was perhaps accidentally transported with trade goods.[11] Recent zoology texts suggests that the reason why the house mouse took so long to reach Britain in comparison to the harvest mouse, which arrived in pre-Neolithic times, was that, unlike other mice, *M. musculus* was better suited to open spaces than forest, and was therefore only able to enter the Mediterranean once agriculture and pastoralism had begun to develop.[12] Contemporary zooarchaeologists consider it most likely that the house mouse entered the Mediterranean Basin sometime between 6,000 and 1,000 BC. Incredibly, given its long history with human populations, however, the house mouse has only been established in Britain for around 2,000 years, since roughly the Iron Age, with no wide distribution until the Saxon-Medieval phases.[13]

Other British mice of the family Muridae include the Eurasian harvest mouse (*Micromys minitus*), the wood mouse or long-tailed field mouse (*Apodemus sylvaticus*) and the closely related yellow-necked mouse (*A. flavicollis*); and of the Gliridae family, the (endangered) common or hazel dormouse (*Muscardinus avellanarius*), which is one of Britain's most endangered mammals, along with the edible dormouse (*Glis glis*), which was accidentally introduced to Tring, Hertfordshire, in 1902 after an escape from Walter Rothschild's zoological collection. The wood mouse is the true 'field mouse', which has become something of a generic term for a number of British mice. Most mice, including the house mouse, are nocturnal and have a heightened sense of danger, which protects them from their countless predators: cats, dogs, owls, crows, kestrels, foxes, stoats, weasels, rats and humans. Those that are active during

A family of house mice nesting in a garden birdhouse.

the daytime, such as harvest mice and wood mice, keep out of our way, lost in open fields and hidden in burrows, thickets, forest edges and hedgerows. The diets of most British mice may include berries, fruits, nuts, bark, leaves, flowers, nectar, seeds, moss and herbaceous products, as well as fungi, snails, insects and human left-overs. House mice in particular, although they prefer cereals, have developed an appetite for a variety of peculiar provisions, includ-ing electrical cables, candles and soap.

So how, then, do we recognize the house mouse? Not all mice found in human habitations are house mice. Particularly in the winter months, wood mice and yellow-necked mice can often be found in homes, sheds and greenhouses. The house mouse grows to between 6.5 and 10 cm from the tip of the nose to the base of the tail, with a tail length of between 5 and 10 cm. It weighs between

12 and 22 g; a heavyweight compared to *Micromys minitus*, or the harvest mouse, which weighs less than half as much. House mice can be identified by their brown-grey coats, large, rounded ears, pronounced muzzles and long tails. The coat of a wood mouse is more orange in tone, and that of a yellow-necked mouse is yellower. Both of these mice have much whiter bellies than the house mouse. House mice live for two years on average but their lifespan can be anything from six months in the wild to five years in captivity. A healthy mouse with a good food supply will produce ten or eleven litters a year, each litter containing no more than fourteen pups, with an average size of six, although some sources claim that litters can range in size from one to 24 young. The gestation period of the house mouse is twenty days, and in some instances the mouse is able to conceive less than a day after giving birth. Female mice (does) are usually on heat every four to five days and ovulate between two and twelve days. One study shows that a doe produces more than sixteen times more milk than a cow per day relative to her body weight.[14] Infant mice mature at between four and eight weeks. Mice are, contrary to popular opinion, extremely clean animals that sometimes even overgroom themselves and other mice, causing bald spots. Many textbooks on house-mouse biology and on keeping mice as pets or for breeding note the animal's aggression, pointing out that males (bucks) fight almost constantly, sometimes to the death. Females are less aggressive than males and even have an aggression inhibitor in their urine. Knowledge of house-mouse aggression is largely based on inbred varieties; little is known of mice in the wild. Recent studies on house-mouse biology suggest that mouse aggression, considered to be largely hereditary and varying from strain to strain, is subjected to natural selection and rapid evolution. House mice are made so successful, then, not only by their physical aptitude to change, but by their social

A mouse represents the secret world in which 'The Borrowers' live: Royal Mail stamp, 1998.

and temporal adaptability. Kept house mice form different hierarchical systems according to their situation and level of confinement, while house mice in the wild – particularly in parts of the world where they have been introduced in relatively recent years, such as the Americas and Australia – cleverly recur in areas and at times when native species, which would be naturally more dominant, are at a low.[15]

If we consider the laboratory mouse, it becomes apparent that the modern evolution of house mice and humans appears to be entwined in terms of the development from simple to more complex forms, the mouse's many manufactured guises functioning as physical representations of increasing human knowledge. In a sense, mice, as models for human disease, mark out the path for human evolution, serving as mirrors into the future of human biology. The house mouse commenced a new

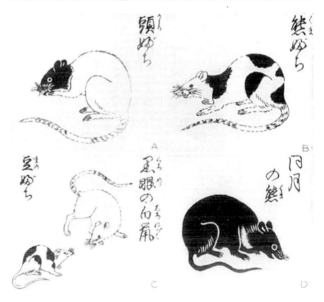

Impressions of mouse mutations from an 18th-century Japanese guide to mouse breeding.

phase in its biological history around the beginning of the twentieth century, when early geneticists in Europe and the United States began using *Mus musculus domesticus, M. m. musculus, M. m. casteneus* and *M. m. bactrianus* from the collections of modern 'mouse fanciers' as test material. The breeding of mice for exhibition, known as mouse fancying, had become popular in Europe around the late nineteenth century; a period of new-found interest in genetics 40 years or so after the publication of Charles Darwin's *On the Origin of Species* (1859). Stocks of ornamental mice were introduced from Japan, where *nezumi* (meaning 'rat' or 'mouse') had been bred for their beauty since the early seventeenth century. A Kyoto money changer, Chobei Zenya, had produced a booklet on the 'breeding of curious varieties of the mouse', *Chinganso-date-gusa*, in 1787, which was introduced to the Western scientific community in 1935 by Dr Mitosi Tokuda as *An Eighteenth Century Japanese Guidebook on Mouse Breeding*. In seventeenth-century Japan mice were bred in a variety of colours that no one had seen before, including 'black', 'white', 'egg-colour', 'pale purple' and 'lilac'.[16] Rats and mice were also bred with various patterns such as 'spotted', 'deer-spotted' and 'cracked-mark'.[17] The title of an earlier text, *Yoso-tama-no-kake-hashi* or 'A Bridge To Obtaining Novel Jewel-like *Nezumi*' (1775), resonates with the modern language used to describe British fancy mice, which seems more suited to precious stones than to animals that are considered dirty and that, in nature, live mostly in the dark: lustrous, rich, sparkling, pure, bright, golden. It emphasizes, as mouse fanciers always do, the absolute disengagement of the exhibition mouse from its feral cousins. The Chinese encyclopaedia the *Erya*, which dates from the end of the Shang Dynasty (1100 BC), suggests a more ancient origin of mouse breeding, referencing mutant varieties that had emerged through years of domestication, such as 'dancing mice' (caused by an inherited neurological condition of the inner ear), 'yellow mice' and mice with what is now referred to by mouse fanciers as 'dominant spotting'.

In the nineteenth century there was no proven law of genetics, although a number of European zoologists bred fancy mice to investigate the results of Galton's theory of ancestral inheritance. The French physiologist W. F. Edwards, in his book *Des Caractères physiologiques des races humaines* (1829), notes how a chemist from Geneva tried a long course of experiments that coupled grey mice with white mice, finding that the offspring were invariably white or grey but never a mixture of both.[18] In 1854 the naturalist J. S. Gaskoin came across a hairless and wrinkled variety of *M. musculus* that had been living in the paper mills of Maidenhead, Berkshire. When the female gave birth to a litter of pups that all shared her abnormality, Gaskoin concluded that like must beget like.[19] The offspring 'rhinoceros mice' were kept in the small-quadruped house in the gardens of the Zoological Society of London. A Mr Clift, in 1820, had found the same kind of mutant mouse in the fireplace of a room in his house and entered it into the Museum of the Royal College of Surgeons' *Catalogue of Monsters*.[20]

Single-gene mutations in fancy mice continued to cause further new traits to appear. Mice with unusual coat types, patterns and colours, as surreal-sounding as Silver, Champagne, Blue, Chocolate and Dove, were favoured for breeding, as were those that exhibited interesting behaviours or defects, such as 'dancing' or 'waltzing' and hairlessness. Mouse stock catalogues of the nineteenth century note varieties such as Red Cream, Ruby-eyed Yellow and Creamy Buff, although white mice, and white mice crossed with black or brown mice, remained popular, selling at around half a crown each in shops in London, or a shilling a pair, according to advertisements in exchange and marts.

'Hickory dickory dock, the mouse ran up the clock . . .', illustration to the English nursery rhyme.

28

HE RAN SWIFTLY UP CLOCK AND SEIZING THE BELL HAMMER STRUCK "ONE,"

It may be that the popularity of the white mouse among fanciers during the first half of Britain's imperial century can be ascribed to the fact that whiteness had strong connotations of purity, superiority and sexual attractiveness. The differing associations of the brown wild mouse to the white domesticated variety seem to echo colonial ideals of race and the civilizing project. A *Boy's Book* of 1855 notes: 'while brown mice can very rarely be tamed, their white cousins are bred and brought up in a state of domestication.'[21]

The wild mouse is not noted for its beauty, and mice, fancy or otherwise, are rarely depicted in art for art's sake. Yet many nineteenth-century naturalists and writers attest to its humble good looks. The American naturalist J. D. Goodman writes: 'the mouse is a very beautiful little animal when not alarmed and at perfect liberty. Its long and slender whiskers which extend in numerous and graceful lines . . . its bright prominent eyes, delicate ears and slight limbs . . . are all such to render it a pleasant and interesting animal.'[22] Another nineteenth-century writer, in a prelude to a children's story about white mice, writes: 'the mouse is a singularly beautiful

A pair of rhino mice with their nest, 1856.

Wood-engraved illustration of a mouse holding court, by John Tenniel from Lewis Carroll's *Alice's Adventures in Wonderland* (1865).

little animal, as no one who examines it attentively and without prejudice can fail to discover.'[23]

In 1892 mice were shown for the first time at a small livestock exhibition in Oxford. Three years later, the popularity of show mice was great enough that Mr Walter Maxey, who became affectionately known as 'the Father of the Fancy', founded the National Mouse Club in East London, with the first mouse show taking place that year in Lincoln. Mouse fanciers travelled with their mice to local and national shows, which awarded small cash prizes to the most unusual specimens.

Today the National Mouse Club sets the breeding standards for around 40 standardized varieties of fancy mice with up to 200 possible variations, to include stipulated shades of eyes, tail and feet. Most varieties of these mice are bred in laboratories and are given two names accordingly: one fancying name and one laboratory name. Fanciers classify mice into the following sections: Selfs, which have one solid colour on top, belly and

An antique thread card showing white mice with satin thread-like white fur-covered tails.

sides; Tan, with a recognized colour on top and a rich tan belly; Marked, patched with a standard colour in combination with white, in various patterns; Satins, which have a high metallic sheen to the coat; and other varieties. These include, among others, Long-haired mice and Astrexes, which have curly coats and whiskers. Exhibition mice are considered stock rather than pets, with surplus, retired, deformed, particularly aggressive and diseased mice culled to save space and money.

The resurgence of scientific interest around 1900 in the Mendelian theory of inheritance, which stated that hereditary characteristics are passed from parent to offspring, enhanced the desire to create further 'new species' of mouse that seemed to defy nature, signifying new knowledge and new possibilities. In 1905, pink-eyed Japanese waltzing mice (*M. m. wagnier*) were bred with existing types, introducing the pink-eye aesthetic to the fancy (not to be confused with the pink eyes of albino mice), which resulted in a number of different colour variations. Further spontaneous mutations continued to emerge, some as a result of radiation, chemical induction or disease. The blue mouse, for example, is an early mutation originally caused by a murine strain of the leukaemia virus.

Early mouse fanciers had unwittingly created genetically homogenous breeds, laying the foundations for momentous scientific discoveries. Geneticists such as the French biologist Lucien Cuénot began using mice from the collections of fanciers just after the turn of the century to demonstrate that Mendel's law applied to mammals and therefore also to humans. The fact that many fancy mice were susceptible to various health defects such as allergies, diabetes, anaemia and proneness to weight gain or the development

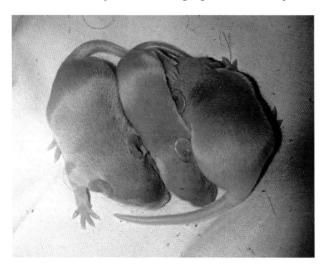

Satin fancy mice.

of tumours eventually made them useful to studies of specific disease. In 1905 scientists at Harvard University began working with tumours in Japanese waltzing mice, concluding that cancer had a genetic basis. Charles C. Little of Harvard, a contemporary of Cuénot, went on to found the Jackson Laboratory in Bar Harbor, Maine, in 1929. He devoted it entirely to research on mammalian genetics and cancer, using the mouse as his fundamental test animal. The National Cancer Institute, founded in 1936, awarded its first grant to the Jackson Laboratory in Maine, which permitted a dramatic increase in research. The laboratory was the first to publish a textbook on the subject, *Biology of Laboratory Mouse* (1941), which was divided into thirteen chapters, five of which were dedicated to cancer biology. After the Second World War two additional

A curly-furred mouse, known by fanciers as a Rex.

to revert to the primitive. This expla[n]
ation seems hardly satisfying.
It now seem[s] improbable that
climate alone is responsible for
the loss of characteristics of bull dogs
for example. In the horse regularily
small forms are obtained on
islands and mountains. This may
be due more to the loss of food
more than climate. Modern knowledge
shows that small horses belong to
a certain breed (Ridgeway) found

Doodles of mice from C. C. Little's Harvard zoology notebook, c. 1910.

major research centres for mouse genetics were established in Britain and the United States in order to study the possible consequences for humans in the event of radiation fallout resulting from an atomic bomb.

In the 1930s mouse breeding became more lucrative. The number of animals used in scientific research in England had risen from 270 in 1879 to 958,761 in 1939, a large proportion of which were mice.[24] Many of these mice were used to test the potency of lethal substances, with one single study on bacterial toxins by J. W. Trevan of the British Wellman Physiology Laboratories deploying 27,000 test subjects.[25] Mice were also used in great numbers in pregnancy testing in the 1930s. The 'reliable' Aschheim-Zondek test, developed in the 1920s by German gynaecologists Selmar Aschheim and Bernhard Zondek, involved the injection of an immature female mouse of around three to four weeks old with the urine of a possibly pregnant woman. Later it was killed and dissected. If the mouse was ovulating then the test was positive. Similar tests were carried out with rabbits and frogs until the

Lynn Randolph, *The Laboratory/ The Passion of the OncoMouse*, 1994, oil on masonite. A Christ-like mouse, sacrificed for humanity.

1950s. Some commercial mouse fanciers of the 1930s also gained from selling their stock to make full-length luxury ladies' coats.

Mice and rats now constitute 90 per cent of the world's research animals, with over 25 million mice being used in scientific experiments across the world at any given moment.[26] The house mouse's remarkable contribution to biomedicine has earned it the title 'hero of science'. Mice have been central to some of the most fundamental medical breakthroughs of the last 50 years, resulting in at least seventeen Nobel Prizes. The rodent's exhaustive list of accolades includes the critical roles it has played in research on immunology, oncology and genetics, and the significant contributions it has made to studies of cancer, Alzheimer's disease and diabetes, and to the development of penicillin and transplant surgery. The house mouse was the first animal model for studies of obesity, and the first patented animal in the world, in the form of the controversial breast-cancer model OncoMouse. Underpinning its status of super-colonizer, the all-penetrative mouse has even been sent on lunar expeditions in studies of osteoporosis that aim to better understand bone disintegration, which occurs naturally in outer space.

The house mouse is used as a surrogate for the human body in studies of almost every imaginable physical and mental ailment, aversion, addiction and negative emotion, as well as in studies of intelligence and memory. It has become a more popular test animal than any other small rodent, including the rat, because of its unrivalled biological similarity to humans. It has been found that mice share 99 per cent of their genes with humans. This, together with the rapid rate at which the mouse propagates, ages and evolves, which makes it possible to breed generations of mice in a very short space of time, means that it can display the future of human disease.

In the 1980s transgenic and knockout technology allowed scientists to create mouse models of human disease by inserting or eliminating certain genes. Highly intelligent Doogie mice were employed for cognitive research on memory and learning, and non-obese diabetic (NOD) mice, first bred in Japan, were generated to develop diabetes mellitus Type One. The knockout Obese mouse was made to eat continuously by knocking out the gene that tells it to stop. Scientists also created the Fearless Mouse using this technology, and the Mighty Mouse, whose disabled myostatin gene is used for studies in muscular dystrophy and other wasting diseases.

Biomedical mice became more and more like figures from a science fiction film; monsters or superheroes that reflected, in their infinite surreal forms, the fears and fantasies of modernity. The first ever patented animal, OncoMouse, genetically engineered for breast cancer research, became a beacon for social anxieties surrounding human interference with nature, causing anger at the almost Cartesian philosophy that animals were no more than soulless inorganic machines. The anthropologist and technoscientist Donna Haraway, together with the artist Lynn Randolph, portray OncoMouse as a sacrificial Christ-like figure that suffers, like all laboratory animals, in the name of human salvation.

In the laboratory science fiction began to seem, as Baudrillard had written in *Simulacrum and Simulacra* (1994), no longer to be anywhere but everywhere – like mice themselves. Laboratory mice provided visions of possible futures where the natural boundaries of human and non-human, and nature and artifice, had become blurred.

In the 1990s 'Humanized Mice' were bred to have human genes, cells, tissues and/or organs. Two types are used, predominantly in studies of the immune system and transplantation: the Nude/Hairless Mouse and the Severe Combined Immunodeficient (SCID) Mouse, the latter possessing a near-complete non-functioning immune system. A mouse known as the Murphy Roth Large (MRL) was discovered in 1999 to possess incredible regenerative capabilities unnatural to other mammals. Produced through ordinary breeding, the MRL mouse is able to recreate lost

or damaged cells, tissues, organs and even limbs in the way that amphibians and starfish do; properties that could be transferred to enhance the regenerative capacity of mammals in general. Trumpeted by the media as the 'Miracle Mouse', MRL is even capable of regrowing hearts.[27] In a 2006 study scientists found a mouse with a natural resistance to cancer. It was discovered that injections of white blood cells from the cancer-resistant mouse could be used to cure other mice of cancer, and the research team has since been granted permission by the U.S. government to search for people with the same resistance to cancer as the 'Super Mouse'. Scientists in the U.S. hope that a mouse gene capable of slowing down the effects of ageing in humans could signal the way for a golden age of humanity.

Dormouse in an apple tree, etching.

In a photograph of the Vacanti Earmouse by Patricia Piccinnini, *Protein Lattice* (1997), a rodent with a human 'ear' protruding revoltingly from its back sits on the shoulder of a seemingly naked woman. The artificial is pictured in a highly glossed hybrid of animal and human, the perfect and the monstrous, the organic and the technological, as the mutated rodent diffuses into the model's skin – mouse and human as one, with one suffering for the other's gain. The 'ear' that caused so much controversy in the press was in fact human cartilage grown in a mould and attached to the mouse in order to study the transplantation of cartilage in humans. This monstrous animal, like a mythological chimera, makes us think of the imagined nightmares of modern science that have come to life in stories such as Mary Shelley's *Frankenstein* (1818) and H. G. Wells's *The Island of Dr Moreau* (1896).

Today 3,000 strains of mice are produced at the Jackson Laboratory alone, and are supplied to 56 countries around the world. Many of these strains have nicknames based on their man-made defects, such as Wobbler, Dancer, Punk Rocker, Ducky, Lethargic, Tottering and Stargazer, a mouse 'detected by its unsteady gait and unusual repeated head-elevations'. On the Jackson Laboratory's website, it is possible to shop online for mice for scientific study. Like buying anything else on the Internet, you select from various options on a dropdown menu before pressing 'Purchase' at the bottom of the page. You can select specific strains to study anything from deafness to dwarfism, obesity to OCD, narcolepsy to night blindness, rheumatoid arthritis to rubinstein tabyi and other rare disorders such as Crigler-Najjar syndrome. The mice can be bought alive or cryopreserved (ready for recovery); and there are countless strains of mice 'not yet available/under development'. Strain 'C.Cg – Tg (DRD1-ctxa) 7Burt / J', for example, is a transgenic mouse that may be useful for studies of compulsive disorders such as Tourette's syndrome and trichotillomania (hair-pulling).

In its laboratory and fancy form, the house mouse has become more a product of culture than nature; and yet however we may come to define and separate those two entities, as if one were the definition of real and the other of artifice, the mouse continues to evolve – and through it, so do we. While we see the mouse as a victim in our laboratories, stock for our exhibitions or a pest in our homes, we should be humbled by this animal to which we owe so much, both for what we have already learned from it and what we will continue to learn in the future. One day the world may be inherited by colourful laboratory mice capable of telekinesis and levitation, while we, as cyborgs, thanks to what we have learned from *M. musculus*, inhabit some other planet.

2 The Mouse in Egypt, Greece and Rome

Stop! Or thou shalt eat the mouse, the abomination of Ra.
Book of the Dead

The mouse in the classical world was both divine and demonic – grand adjectives for the so-called *ridiculus mus*. In Egypt and Greece the mouse was conceived of as a punishment from or weapon of the gods; connected, like other dangerous and uncontrollable natural forces, to the destructive side of the divine. Yet it was also held sacred in its own right, and became a positive symbol and totem animal of a number of cult deities throughout the classical world. A great paradox, the mouse was a creature of life and death, the earth and the underworld, light and dark, and the sun and the moon; feted for its connection to immortality, prophecy and magic.

On the agricultural coasts of the Mediterranean, the animals most likely to be revered were typically those that most influenced the crop. It was then inevitable that the mouse, which had the power to destroy it in its entirety, would possess great divine significance in ancient Egypt, Greece and Rome. The development of towns and pastoralism in the classical world can be held largely responsible for the spread of the house mouse into the western Mediterranean, offering the mouse food, shelter and protection from predators.[1]

Some of the oldest records of mouse infestations derive from Petrie in Egypt, where rodent tunnelling was found in nearly every room of the houses in the twelfth-dynasty town at Kahun and in the fortress town of Buhen, both dating from 1700 BC.[2] The Egyptians caught mice in traps and plugged their holes with stones. As well as the cat, they deployed the mongoose, known as the Pharaoh's mouse, to catch mice. (The domestication and deification of cats – and mongooses – in Egypt and beyond can largely be attributed to the problem of the mouse.) The Greeks used the *Myagros* snake, meaning 'mouser' or 'mousetrap', to defend against rodents. Together with the Romans they also adopted the weasel for the same purpose, and later the cat. Classical mouse plagues of catastrophic destruction were recorded by the Greek and Roman scholars Strabo, Aelian, Pliny, Diodorus Siculus and Theophrastus.[3] The last wrote that the Greek island of Gyaros was so overrun by field mice that the inhabitants were forced to flee.[4]

Of course, not all rodents shared the same meaning in the ancient world, although is it still the case that 'mouseness' was a much broader concept to which various species could have contributed. As well as house mice (subspecies *musculus, bactrianus,*

Jerboas with a backdrop of pyramids, in M.H.C. Lichtenstein's book of natural history, *Säugethiere* (1827–34).

Tab. XXII.

43

praetextus, *orientalis* and *domesticus*), field mice (*M. macedonicus*; *M. spretus*; *M. spicilegus*) and various species of jerboas, spiny mice, wood mice, harvest mice and dormice, there were shrews, voles, rats, mole-rats, hamsters, gerbils, weasels, ermines, martens, sables, hyraxes, and even porcupines and hedgehogs (and moles, which aren't rodents at all); many of which are also burrowing, mostly nocturnal, relatively small and/or have similar, mainly herbivorous diets. Some more visually striking murine species were referenced specifically in art, artefacts and myths. Illustrations of the jerboa, for example, were common in Egypt. The British Museum holds a pink stamp from southern Mesopotamia dating from 4000–3000 BC with a jerboa and a star on its back. The jerboa seems to have had a special kind of significance in the Bible lands, too. Some commentators of the Old Testament attribute the name of the mouse in the Bible, *ackbar* – which can be rendered as 'destruction of the corn' – specifically to the jerboa. However, given that the jerboa is typically shy and desert-dwelling,

Mice caught in traps.

it is much more likely that *ackbar* was used to describe mice and mouse-like creatures in general, tarring them all with the brush of the notorious field mouse. The *ackbar* is referred to in the Book of Isaiah (66:17) as having been eaten ceremoniously by ancient Mesopotamians; perhaps, as the nineteenth-century anthropologist James G. Frazer puts it in his famous text *The Golden Bough* (1890), as 'the body and blood of gods'. The Book of Isaiah also mentions idolatrous mouse eating: 'They who sanctify themselves and purify themselves in the gardens . . . eating swine's flesh, the abomination, and the mouse, shall be consumed together, saith the Lord.'

The jerboa later featured prominently in European natural history books of the eighteenth and nineteenth centuries as a sort of exotic national mouse of Egypt; it was often pictured, as if enormous, in the foreground of pyramid landscapes. Aristotle had previously taught that all mice in Egypt walked on two legs and were covered in hedgehog-like quills,[5] an idea inspired by fused impressions of the jerboa and the spiny mouse. Often naturalists applied a characteristic distinct to one type of mouse to the entire family. The shrew or shrew-mouse's venomous bite, for example, was a trait considered shared by mice in general. The shrew-mouse was distinguished by its elongated snout. Many references to the sacred mouse of Egypt specify the shrew, and it is immortalized in a great number of ancient Egyptian artefacts. Despite its unique appearance, symbolically it corresponded to a general idea of 'mouse'. The blind mole-rat, plump with outsized teeth and a bulbous snout, also made an impression; it may have contributed to the classical belief that all mice were sightless. It is also probable that the mole-rat in some places played a part in murine divinity. The ancient Greek poem on hunting, *Cynegetica*, describes an 'earth-born tribe' of blind and gluttonous mole-rats that sprang from the blood of an angry king.[6]

Book illustration of a fountain composed of mice, in the labyrinth in the gardens at Versailles, c. 1670s.

The nineteenth-century writer Andrew Lang, in his *Custom and Myth* (1884), draws attention to a mouse myth set on Egyptian soil that attempted to justify the worship of a beast as 'undignified' as the mouse.[7] The myth, narrated by the ancient Greek historian Herodotus (*c.* 484–*c.* 425 BC), tells of a priest and king of Egypt, Sethos, who, when he found himself without an army on Sennacherib's invasion of his country, was sent a message as he slept in the temple, telling him that the Egyptians would receive divine succour. The night before the battle, Sethos was avenged by field mice that gnawed the quivers and shield-handles of the enemy, leaving the opposition disarmed and Egypt victorious. Herodotus notes how a stone image of this king, with a mouse in his hand, stands in the temple of Hephaestus with the inscription 'Let whoso looketh on me be pious.' It has been suggested that Sethos was a representation of Ptah, god of regeneration, fertility and the sun, who came before Ra. (The story is thought by some scholars to be a version of a biblical account, 2 Samuel 18–19, of the destruction of Sennacherib's army, supposedly by pestilence in 701 BC, although this is often contested.) As in many mouse tales, the rodent is presented as a divine avenger that uses its destructive qualities for good – as far as the Egyptians were concerned. Mice appear in this way in a great number of ancient and modern texts. Perhaps the most famous of these stories is Aesop's fable 'The Lion and the Mouse' – and modern allusions to it, such as C. S. Lewis's *The Lion, the Witch and the Wardrobe* (1950) – wherein mice gnaw ropes to set free sacred lions. The need to avert the destruction represented by the mouse formed the very basis of its worship.

The sanctification of the mouse sought predominantly to appeal to the rodent's better nature in an effort to protect valuable grain. Mouse deities were typically gods of fertility and agriculture who both adored the mouse and guarded against it. It is for this reason that many mouse gods display aspects of the predator, particularly in Egypt, where they are either characteristically depicted in animal form (that is, entirely in animal form, as in the case of Wadjet and the snake, or with the head of the animal, as with Ra and the hawk) or paired with them in myth: the cat with Ra and Isis (and, in Greece, with Artemis/Diana); the hawk with Ra and Horus; and the snake with Wadjet. (In Akkadian and Sumerian mythology, too, the mouse is connected to a harvest deity and eagle god who is given the epithet *humsiru*, meaning 'Lord of the Mouse'.) While the predator represented sacred protection against the mouse, the image of this tiny rodent and its antithesis at the same time signified the great universal cycle

A section of an ancient Egyptian papyrus satirizing society during the reigns of the last Ramesside kings, showing a cat waiting on a mouse, along with other animals in reversal of the natural order. Twentieth Dynasty (about 1186–1069 BC), possibly from Deir el-Medina.

of life and death, and the creative and destructive powers of the gods. The shrew-mouse and the mongoose were a symbolic pair, each one swelling to the size of the other, like the sun and the moon. Many gods connected to the mouse (Ptah, Ra, Apollo) were also gods of light, the perfect weapon against the nocturnal mouse. The worship of the mouse was also a means of penetrating its divine wisdom. It was believed throughout the classical world that because the mouse could destroy the crop, it possessed mystical control over the yield. It was, then, by its very nature, conceived of as a creature in possession of prophetic power.

In ancient Egypt the mouse was considered divine in its own right but was also sacred to the deities Ra, Isis, Horus, Djehuty and Wadjet. According to the Greek geographer Strabo (*c.* 63 BC–*c.* AD 24), the shrew-mouse was venerated independently in the Egyptian city of Crocodilopolis.[8] Animal cults still subsisted in Egypt in the Late Dynastic and Graeco-Roman periods. Many of the mouse's roles in Egyptian culture are not at all unlike those he plays today. Toy mice made of painted clay, some set on wheels, have been uncovered from Egyptian sites. Relics depicting coloured mice suggest that mice were also bred as objects of fancy and kept as pets. In art, predominantly from the Ramesside Period (Nineteenth and Twentieth Dynasties), anthropomorphic mice were comic characters in original satirical cat-and-mouse stories that portrayed mice as pharaohs who fight, triumph over, enslave and are subsequently fanned and attended to by cats. Baby mice have cats for housemaids; male mice are shown wearing kilts, which were objects of high status; and servant cats wait on upper-class lady mice.

Despite their humour, the Egyptians were superstitious. They are said to have believed that mice were spontaneous products of the Nile mud, for each year, when the river flooded, a terrible plague of mice appeared as if by magic. Emerging from the riverbanks in their thousands, crusted in soil, mice appeared to be

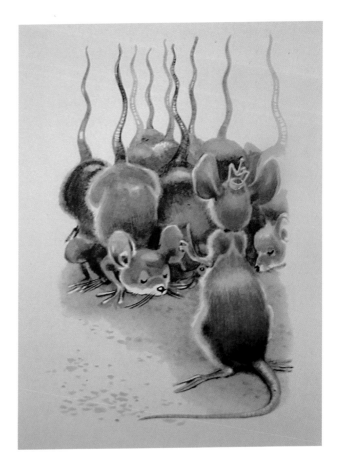

Book illustration of the 'Queen of the Field Mice' from L. Frank Baum's *The Wonderful Wizard of Oz.*

composed half of flesh and half of mud. It is likely to be for this reason that Isidore of Seville later suggested a connection between the Latin words *humus* (mud) and *mus* (mouse).[9] A number of classical and early Christian scholars wrote of these mice, including Pliny the Elder, who noted in his *Natural History* that when the Nile's inundation recedes, 'minute mice are to be discovered in a state in which . . . part of their body is alive [and] the extremity is still a cast of earth.'[10] The mouse was synonymous with the earth, for it existed at its level, was prolific in its fields and issued from its holes.

However, owing to its dual residence above and below the surface of the earth, it was equally connected to imaginings of the underworld. As a creature that was only half flesh and that emanated from beneath the ground, the mouse was regarded as a supernatural mediator between the worlds of the living and the dead. Mice could often be seen emerging from corpses, which led the Egyptians to believe that they were the escaping souls of the deceased. The mouse was sometimes portrayed as the guardian of souls. In some versions of the Book of the Dead, the kingdom of death is guarded by a goddess with the head of a mouse. Deities with murine heads were also depicted in tombs such as that of Nefertari, the favourite royal wife of Ramesses the Great. Since the mouse took away life (and yet created it so miraculously among its own kind) it was believed to be able to restore it. The image of a mouse emerging from its burrow was also symptomatic of the

African pygmy mouse.

creative transition from darkness to light. As such, the symbol of the mouse, as W. J. Loftie tells us in his *Essay on Scarabs* (1884), was sometimes used in place of that of the divine beetle, as an amulet for resurrection, buried with the dead.[11] Other creatures that took the place of the scarab in this way were often those that, like the mouse, emerged from the fertile waters of the Nile, such as the hippopotamus and the frog. (The relationship between the mouse and water will be explored later in the context of ancient Greece.) Twelfth- and Thirteenth-Dynasty figures of jerboas and frogs uncovered from a vaulted tomb in Heliopolis are now kept at the Fitzwilliam Museum at the University of Cambridge. A bronze knife handle in the form of a mouse from the British Museum may have been used in Egyptian funerary rites. During Opening of the Mouth Ceremonies, the mouths of the deceased were opened to allow them symbolically to eat and drink in the afterlife; an act carried out in the name of Ptah, 'the Opener'. Although usually a serpent-handled blade was used, it is possible that this murine knife was used in the same way (especially as the mouse was a symbol of the mouth – the great devourer), although there is no evidence to back this up. Mice were also heralded as a means of restoring life to the dying. Forcing mice down the throats of the deceased, or those in their last extremity, was a means of putting the soul, and particularly the child soul, back into the body before or as it tried to escape. The Egyptologist Warren R. Dawson records in *The Bridle of Pegasus* (1930) how, in 1901, the partial carcasses of skinned mice were found in the alimentary canals of children's bodies dating from the fourth millennium BC.[12]

The souls of the mice themselves were also important to the Egyptians, who mummified the tiny animals in death. The bound rodents were often gifts to the cat goddess Bastet, with countless tiny mummies found buried in cats' tombs in Thebes. However, like other mummified creatures in Egypt, embalmed mice also functioned as intermediaries between humans and gods, and were preserved to ensure their eternal destiny. Mummified mice were placed in their own, often embellished containers. A bronze one with a sculpture of a shrew on its lid is kept at the British Museum.

The English scholar Harold Walter Bailey declares in his fascinating book *The Lost Language of Symbolism* (1968) that the word soul in almost every language takes its meaning from the Sun or from the Great Light of God.[13] It is then fitting that the mouse, as a zootype of the soul, was held sacred in the first instance to Ra, the Sun and the Creator, god of rebirth, light and growth. When the Sun descended into the Egyptian underworld it was imagined as a disappearing mouse – the symbol of Ra – which, on re-emerging, signified rebirth and the eternal soul. Ra, who was known to travel in his Sun Boat with Sia (Perception) and Heka (Magic), reflected the prophetic qualities of the professed crop-governing mouse.

The Egyptians later connected the mouse with the moon, 'the source of fertility and the measurer of days of man'. The livers of mice have been recorded in a number of ancient and early modern European texts as waxing and waning with the moon. The Egyptians noticed that the 28 teeth of the shrew-mouse mirrored the number of days in each lunar phase. The mouse consequently became sacred to the son and scribe of Ra, Djehuty, god of the moon, magic and knowledge. While Djehuty is famously depicted as a baboon, iconography of the god shows the mouse sitting at the base of his wand or 'rod of destiny'. As the moon became linked more with the female than the male through its connection to the 28-day menstrual cycle, the mouse became more heavily associated with the goddess. It is probably worth mentioning here that one of the earliest suggestions of the mouse's connection to goddess worship in the ancient Near East derives from a region north of Mesopotamia in the Neolithic settlement of Çatal Hüyük

(*c.* 7500–5700 BC) in what is now Turkey, where an important woman uncovered from a shrine had been buried wearing a necklace of mouse bones. The Egyptian mother goddess and goddess of the moon, fertility and magic, Isis, is known to have had the mouse as her totem. Isis' virgin blood was regarded in Egypt as the soul of life, and was represented by the red mouse. This red mouse subsequently became consecrated in the image of the soul born of Isis' blood, the Child-Horus. Horus, god of light, became a particularly eminent shrew god with a mouse-cult centre in the Egyptian city of Panopolis. He was particularly important in the development of the mouse as a symbol of the child soul, the servant and blindness within and beyond Egypt. The mouse, deemed blind by the Egyptians, was thus a fitting totem for Horus, who as a mortal servant child was also sightless; a connotation of the obscurity prior to spiritual enlightenment, and the journey from mortality to immortality. The mouse continued to be sacred to Horus in his eternal aspect, associated chiefly with the god's dark side.

A creature of purported blindness, the mouse is associated in myth and ancient medicine with the restoration of sight. When Horus was blinded by the Black Set Pig, his sight was restored by the mouse-god Djehuty. A similar myth of Horus and Djehuty accounts for the mouse's use as a cure for scorpion stings in the classical world. In ancient Egyptian papyri there are several references to the medicinal use of mice. Dried dead mouse beaten into a powder together with the liver of ducks and frogs, for example, was commonly used in relieving kidney disease.[14] The mouse was also believed, owing to his own supreme teeth, to be a fine cure for toothache, as part of a system of ancient sympathetic magic. The mouse is depicted in paintings of the first recorded 'dentist', Hesi-Re, from 2600 BC. (In many European cultures the 'Tooth Fairy' is instead the 'Tooth Mouse'.) There is also a story from

Gustave Doré's engraving of La Fontaine's fable 'The Town Mouse and the Country Mouse'.

the Old Testament that is particularly significant to the mouse as an object of healing in the ancient Near East, connecting the rodent to Dagon, an Assyro-Babylonian fertility god. It relates how, when the Philistines had captured the Ark of the Covenant and set it in the house of Dagon, the people, covered in swellings or emerods from plague, were instructed to make images of both the emerods and of 'the mice that mar the land' so as to 'give glory unto the God of Israel'. It is also worth mentioning the use of mice as remedies against miscarriage in Babylonia. A clay magico-medical tablet from between 400 and 600 BC, kept at the British Museum, gives a prescription against the loss of an unborn child. The text recommends that the woman wear a particular species of dried edible mouse stuffed with myrrh for three days – the offering to the child.

Finally in Egypt, the mouse was venerated by Wadjet, goddess of prophecy and the personification of the famous eye of Horus. Wadjet's illustrious oracle is likely to have been the source of the oracular tradition which spread from ancient Egypt to Greece, taking the prophetic mouse with it. Originally solar, Wadjet was made lunar by the Greeks, for whom she became known as Leto (Buto). She was considered to be the mother of Apollo (the Greek Horus), and was the idol of one of the most eminent and worthy mouse cults in history. Bronze mice can be found at Wadjet's cult centre Letopolis, some inscribed with the prayers of pilgrims.[15] Mummified shrew-mice (together with the mongoose) have also been found in statuettes of the goddess. The Greek-named city of Letopolis shares its hieroglyph with that of the lightning bolt, an image with which the Greeks associated the darting mouse. Giuseppe Angelo De Gubernatis, in his *Zoological Mythology* (1872), notes how the Aryans also visualized lightning as the flashing tooth of a mouse.[16] A weapon of the gods and sign of phallic power, lightning was present during fertile rains, which brought prolific mice in great numbers. (Fittingly, one of the mouse's predators, the owl, was thought in ancient Greece to give divine protection against lightning.)

In ancient Greece the mouse was no longer held sacred in his own right, but instead was a divine symbol associated with Apollo, Demeter, Persephone and Dionysus. The Greeks held ceremonial mouse feasts in Rhodes, Gela, Lesbos and Crete to ensure long life, continuing to regard the mouse as a being of immortality and a measurer of days.

The prophetic mouse moved from Egyptian magic to the Greek mystery. In *Rhetoric* of *c.* 400 BC Aristotle notes how mice were fundamental to the most honourable rites and mysteries.[17] Aelian referred to them, in his *Varied Histories* of *c.* AD 300, as the most prophetic of all animals. Their shrieking and dancing were deemed portentous of storms and heavy rains. Theophrastus wrote about mice eating iron in Cyprus, and gold among the Chalybes peoples of Turkey, for which the rodents were cut open in mines.[18] The mouse became so suggestive of mystery that one scholar even argues that the word 'mystery' itself is derived from the word for mouse.[19] The prefix of the Greek word for 'mystery', *mus'terion*, is of course the Indo-European *mus*. *Mys* in 'mystery' also means 'mouse' or 'mice' as well as 'quest for knowledge'. It lends itself to an epithet of the mouse goddess Demeter, Mys'ia. Demeter is Isis' Greek counterpart, a harvest goddess and earth mother. She is pictured with a mouse, probably a harvest mouse, and an ear of barley on a number of coins from Metapontum in Italy dating from the end of the classical or beginning of Hellenistic times, around the fourth to fifth century BC. The general meaning of 'mystery' derives from *myo*, also meaning 'mouse' in ancient Greek, but can alternatively be translated as 'to keep one's eyes and mouth shut'.[20] The mouse was an obvious zootype for the mystery given that it was synonymous with secret knowledge, and that in Greek rituals it was associated with being both blind and mute.[21] (The prefix *mys* also means '*mus*-cle', which may have phallic significance or refer to a moving muscle appearing like a mouse under the skin. We know this is not a coincidence because it is also true of the Arabic, where *adalah* ('muscle') is prefixed by *adal* ('field mouse').

The mouse was sacred to Demeter's daughter Persephone, goddess of the underworld, and to her son Dionysus, a fallen soul and a communicator between the living and the deceased. In Greek literature mice are depicted as souls of the dead or guides to the underworld. In a Hellenistic fable, Glaucus, son of Minos and Pasiphae, is brought back to life with herbs after falling into a jar of honey and dying while pursuing a mouse. Honey was considered an offering to underworld deities, and, in a jar big enough to drown a man, became a sort of symbolic gateway to Hades. The Cretan poet Bergadis (*c.* 1400) paints an apocalyptic picture of two mice – 'fat, sleek, and as big as pigs' – that lick the spillings from the beard of a disgusting old man as he devours his underworld meal of cabbage and bacon.[22] The Greeks believed that mice lived and multiplied in Hades, only occasionally visiting the living by springing up from small cracks in the earth's surface.[23] In this way mice were held in a similar symbolic category to fungi. The mouse, like the mushroom (Latin: *mus'cinae*, 'moss'), appeared after storms, and, like fungi, was deemed a parasitic, abundant, mysterious, dangerous and divine mediator with the otherworld. Some types of fungus have even been named after the mouse, such as the 'mouse tricholoma' and the 'mouse-skin byssus'. *Mus* was also symptomatic of other pests that reproduced rapidly, such as the fly (Latin *mus'ca*) and mosquito (*mus'quito*). Aristotle regarded the mouse as the most prolific of beasts, suggesting that one pregnant mouse closed in a jar would produce more than 120 mice.[24] He also claimed that in some parts of Persia, when pregnant mice were dissected, the embryos were found to be pregnant.[25] He also taught that a single lick between mice could result in pregnancy and that in Abyssinia mice were able to multiply merely by licking salt.[26] In ancient Greece a few drops of a potion made from the dung of a mouse, applied by a woman to her lover's genitalia, were believed to quell his sexual desires, or even in some instances to cause his impotency. Because of its fecundity the mouse was symbolic of genitalia. The ancient Greek playwright Epicrates instead describes a lustful woman as a *myonia*, or mousehole.[27]

The mouse was sacred in Greece most of all to Apollo, god of wisdom, prophecy, disease, healing, fertility, light and the sun. In the *Iliad* he is referred to as Apollo *Smintheus*, 'Lord of Mice' or 'Mouse Apollo'. This title was bestowed upon him for ridding the Troad of a plague of mice – or for punishing the mice that devastated Chryse, depending on what you read. Apollo *Smintheus* derives his name from *sminthus*, meaning 'mouse', which is also related to *smin*, or *simon*: 'semen', 'the soul fire', 'the seed'. Andrew Lang tells us how an effigy in the Trojan town of Chrysa shows Apollo with a mouse beneath his foot. The idol of the mouse was preserved in Apollo's *sminthiac* temples where white mice dwelt beneath the altars and were fed at public expense. Votive offerings of mice have been discovered in the Greek acropolis of Argos in Larissa, and also in East Peloponnese. The Argives (Argos) stamped the mouse on their coins, and according to Strabo and Homer, towns in the Troad took their names from *sminthus*, or 'mouse'. Strabo notes how the worship of the Mouse Apollo extended to the whole coasts of Asia Minor and the neighbouring islands.[28] Rhodes, Lindos, Caressus and Poeessa were also once centres of *sminthiac* tribes. On the Greek islands we find an Ionian settlement known as Myonnesus, or Pondikónisi in modern Greek, meaning Mouse Island; and on another island a *pondikókastro*, or mouse castle. There was also apparently a city of Ionia (in what is now Anatolia in Turkey) called Myes, after 'mice', which may or may not have had anything to do with a mouse cult.

Apollo *Smintheus* is portrayed in a robe of mouse skins. Like the blindness of Horus, this unenviable garment reflects the god's humble position of servitude prior to enlightenment and immortality. Out of love for Apollo, the Scythians (Iranian nomads) also wore the skins of mice; and, in many European tales from the nineteenth century, so too did the popular heroine Cinderella. Cinderella is interpreted by experts in mythology as the virginal 'maiden' form of the Triple Goddess. Cinderella appears to physically embody the Lord of Mice in a number of variants by being robed in a mouse-skin mantle, which the Prince casts off to reveal her majesty. In several early versions of the tale the heroine is called '(Little) Mouse Skin', and popular adaptations of the eighteenth century are entitled 'The Girl Clad in Mouse Skin' or 'The Girl in the Mouse-skin Cloak'.[29] In numerous tales Cinderella catches mice and hangs their skins on sticks; she fashions a cloak from the skins to disguise her regal identity before being forced to work as a servant. In one variant Cinderella demands from her father four dresses as a payment for agreeing to marry: a sky-blue dress with stars, one silver, one gold and one made from the skins of mice. Another of Apollo's names, *Eleleus*, shares the same root as that of Cinderella: *Ele*, shiner or giver of light.[30] The heroine is a custodian of fertility who is sometimes described as 'The Hearth Cat'.[31] Like Cinderella, Artemis, Apollo's twin sister, is a cat goddess and goddess of the moon and agriculture who, like her brother, drove away mice. It may be worth mentioning here that the transformation of the mice into noble steeds in *Cinderella* reflects the symbolic relationship between the mouse and the horse, as creatures of the moon, the decider of destiny. The Arcadians are said to have sacrificed mice and white horses to the gods. Horses are obviously creatures of war, and mouse plagues often appear like armies. (In Babylonia, mice were important metaphors for invading armies and stealthy enemies. In the Babylonian *Epic of Gilgamesh* of *c.* 2500 BC, when a character resembling Hercules, Ea-bari, comes to the aid of the besieged city of Erech, the gods turn into flies and the spirits into mice, quickly escaping into holes.)

Perhaps the mouse's finest (or let's say 'most famous') moment in Greek culture was in the Homeric hymn *The Battle of the Frogs and the Mice*, or *Batrachomyomachia*. This tongue-twister of a battle is an allusion to the Greek epics, which might also be interpreted as a war of fertility. Figurines of both the frog and the mouse in depictions of the battle at Athribis have been given unnaturally large phalluses.

The tale of *Batrachomyomachia* begins with a frog king known as 'Puff-cheeks' (Physignathus) who attempts to befriend a mouse, 'Crumb-filcher' (Psicharphax), who is drinking from the pond. Puff-cheeks admires Crumb-filcher's warrior-like appearance, and invites him to his kingdom. After some persuasion, Crumb-filcher accepts Puff-cheeks's offer and climbs onto his back, but a snake comes along, the frog dives under the water and the mouse drowns. When questioned by the Crumb-filcher's family, Puff-cheeks denies that the incident ever took place, so the mice wage war on the frogs. The mice are so destructive that Zeus is forced to send an army of crabs to prevent the complete obliteration of the amphibians. Unable to overcome the power of the crabs' shattering claws (or mouths, according to Homer), the mice retreat, and the war ends at sundown. The frog, like the mouse, is a symbol of fertility, believed to be a product of the Nile's inundation. However, generally speaking (although he has been sent as a plague), he is less destructive to the land than the mouse. The names of the mice in the story reflect the mouse's habit of feeding

An *askos*, anointer
or baby feeder
in the shape
of a mouse,
c. 450–425 BC.

on that which others have provided: Pot-stalker, Lick-meal, Cheese-scooper, and One Who Follows the Steam of the Kitchen. The crab is relevant in that, apart from being an avenger in ancient Greece, he casts out his shells as he outgrows them and therefore also has to do with ideas of rebirth and fertility. The crab acts as a protective castrator, chopping off the hands, feet and tails of the mice. In conjunction with his fertility symbolism, the crab is particularly meaningful as the slayer of the impure mouse because of his relationship to the purifying waters of the sea.

The mouse has an ancient symbolic relationship to water. The mouse was believed at one time to have emanated from the vapours of the earth, and from the lakes, rivers and fountains of Arcadia. We recall how the mouse's liver is thought to wax and wane with the lunar phases, as apparently do the ovaries of sea urchins. It has already been noted that mice were believed to be born of the Nile and brought by heavy rains. We also find many harbours named after mice because the rodents descended there from boats in great numbers. An ancient one existed on the Red Sea, Myos Hormos or 'Mouse Harbour'. It makes sense that the fertile and prophetic mouse is connected to water, and ultimately to the sea, as a symbol of new life and the wisdom of the deep. Of course this relationship might also have something to do with the lakes and rivers of the underworld, of bodies of water so deep that they lead to Hades.

A Greek askos, or pottery vessel, from the Leo Mildenberg Collection, offers an interesting example of the mouse's ancient relationship to water. The askos (*c.* 425–400 BC) is formed in the shape of a mouse, and is embellished with silhouettes of octopi on both sides, their eight tentacles outstretched as if floating out of the funnel on the mouse's back. This pottery vessel is believed

A 'Lobster jockey' unites the mouse with the sea in this greetings card, 1880s.

to have been used as a baby feeder, and the curators have suggested that it had something to do with the cult of Apollo or Demeter. No explanation, however, is given for the relationship between the mouse and the sea creature. The relevance of the octopus to this askos, and in turn to the mouse more generally, lies initially in its number of legs, and secondly in its relationship to the sea. The number eight is an ancient symbol of regeneration sacred to Djehuty, who was not only 'the regenerator who poured the waters of purification on the heads of the initiated',[32] but also, of course, a mouse god. The image of the mouse in the askos probably functioned as some kind of symbol of or talisman against infantile disease, while the octopus acted as an embodiment of the protective and purifying qualities of the sea and its salt. Images of sea creatures depicted alongside mice serve to symbolically neutralize the dangers that are embodied in the mouse. Some millennia later we see a Victorian greetings card of circa 1880 on which a mouse holding a scroll scrawled with the words '*Paix, Joie, Santé, Bonheur*' is riding upon a lobster, wishing the beneficiary 'Peace, Joy, Health and Happiness'.

Lastly we turn to ancient Rome, which was shaken by a number of plagues. Here the mouse's most significant role was as a portent for and symbol of death and destruction. Yet children also kept mice as pets. Mice featured prominently in Roman art. Small bronze mice (often dormice), typically shown nibbling nuts, were popularly deployed as apotropaic images to guard food stores between the first and third centuries BC. The mouse features alongside Mercury on a Gallo-Roman relief, either as an omen or as a protector, referencing the god's connection to the grain trade. In funerary sculpture bronze mice appear on tomb lamps, sitting on their haunches and gnawing at morsels. Painted mice are also abundant on the walls of Etruscan tombs dating from around 300 BC, with one tomb, La Tomba del Topolino, even dedicated entirely to a mouse. In this instance mice probably served as guardians of souls, as they had in Egypt. Perhaps, however, they were simply signs of death and the underworld. Mice appear to a similar effect in Roman fable, gnawing at the roots of the tree of life and causing men clutching onto their branches to fall to their deaths.

Mice and rats were considered such important evil omens in Rome that they had their own form of divination. Myomancy, which some writers consider the most ancient form of fortune

A 15th-century Roman floor tile by Antonio dei Fideli, the colours and intricate patterns of which are designed to keep away mice.

A white mouse and a black mouse, representative of day and night, gnawing at the roots of the Tree of Life, from a Carthusian miscellany of c. 1450–1500.

telling, was dependent entirely on the movements, cries and 'prophetic gnawing' of rodents, and was taken very seriously among the Romans. Mice are said to have foretold the first civil war in Rome by prophetically gnawing the gold in the temple. The Roman scholar Varo asserted that Consul Fabius Maximus resigned from his post due to a warning from rats and mice. The Roman statesman Cato the Elder (234–149 BC), however, was not quite so superstitious. When asked by a troubled man whose slippers had been eaten by mice if he thought it was an omen, Cato famously replied that it certainly was not, and would only have been one had the slippers eaten the mice.[33]

The Romans are known to have eaten mice to ensure long life, as the Greeks had. At special banquets they served jugged dormouse fattened on nuts, stuffed with forcemeat of pork and pounded with pepper, nuts and broth.[34] Pottery jars with internal runways and breathing holes in which dormice were reared, known as *gliraria*, were found at Pompeii. A sort of 'dwelling' or 'fattening' jar, the word *gliraria* is taken from the same verb as the dormouse himself, *gliscere* meaning 'to swell', because the Romans thought that sleep made the dormouse fat. In another recipe mice were dipped in honey, the food of the immortals, and rolled in poppy seeds, a product of narcotics. These ingredients were particularly meaningful to long life when associated with the dormouse, which on waking from long periods of hibernation was imagined as returning, at least symbolically, from death. This species of dormouse (*Glis glis*) became known, as it is today, as the edible dormouse.

Pliny also wrote about the medicinal power of the mouse. He recommended that two mice be swallowed whole every month as a preventative for toothache, and advocated that the ashes of mice be mixed with honey as a remedy for earache, or rubbed directly onto the teeth to sweeten the breath.[35] Mouse blood or a cut-open mouse applied to the skin was deemed an excellent antidote for all kinds of warts; and when burned alive, mice were thought to be good for ulcers on the feet.[36] According to Pliny, the gall of a mouse with vinegar was an advisable remedy for the common problem of extracting an insect from the ear.[37]

We do not see the mouse heavily associated with deities in ancient Rome. Its association with the gods seems by then to have been purely metaphorical. However, the mouse does appear in some early medieval Italian folktales that resonate with classical mythology. The mouse evokes feminine prophecy in a story of the cat goddess Diana, the Roman Artemis, in which the goddess creates the world by filling the bladder of an ox with mice and earth, and blowing into it until it bursts. The mice then become the stars and the rain, and Diana the queen of witches.[38]

Mice in the ancient world were complex and contradictory, divided between the natural and the supernatural; the ordinary and the extraordinary; the friend and the enemy – just as they are today. Many of the mouse's ancient roles are familiar to us: the mouse as a pest, a pet, a toy, a hero, a character in satire. Those that are less so – the mouse as a creature of wisdom, magic and immortality – are more important in our contemporary world than we realize.

3 The Asian Mouse

The mouse is his [Ganesha's] vehicle, glorious for all to behold.
Swami Karpatri, *Shri Bhagavati tattva*

Surprisingly the mouse is mainly absent from Asian art, often overshadowed by the rat, or by animals that are considered more magnificent, beautiful or divine, such as the elephant, cow, buffalo, monkey, lion, tiger, panda, peacock, parrot, crane, hare, horse and goldfish. In one Indian composite image of a camel, mice are used to form the feet, unconsciously marking the animal's place in the pecking order of creatures worth depicting in art. Usually when mice *are* shown, it is with other animals, typically cats or elephants, illustrating scenes from popular folktales, or portraying comedy moments with political undertones or moral advice. In a Japanese *Otsu-e* folk painting from the early eighteenth century a mouse watches a foolish cat get drunk on sake, which it drinks from a large lacquered bowl. The text warns that drinking too much will bring bad luck. (In other versions of the painting it is the mouse that drinks the rice wine instead of the cat, so we cannot give the mouse any credit for being sensible.) Of course it is also true that, as a particularly small animal, the mouse is often difficult to recreate in certain media, or simply not interesting enough. It is probably for this reason that where mice *are* represented they are often made to look much larger than they are, and therefore we sometimes perceive them as (giant) rats. It is perhaps because of its small size that the mouse barely features in Indian stone sculpture, in which so much of the country's fauna

An 18th-century anonymous
Otsu-e folk painting of a
cat and mouse drunk on
sake, following a popular
comic theme.

Mice are the feet of
this composite camel
in a 19th-century
Punjabi watercolour.

Shiva and his family,
his son Ganesha
on his lap and
Ganesha's vehicle
behind them
to our left.

is represented. The exception to this rule is a rock carving depicting a lively scene from a famous fable, the 'Story of the Mice', at Mammalapuram in Tamil Nadu, dating from the seventh to eighteenth centuries. The story tells of a cat (or a jackal in the Buddhist version) who eases some neighbouring mice into a false sense of security by pretending to be an ascetic. The mice are sculpted in various positions in the rock, with one standing on its hind legs, watching the cat practise yoga. The mice are particularly large, and have a muscular form that once again makes them appear more like rats.

It is true that most of the murine symbolism in Asia pertains to the rat. The Chinese famously pay tribute to the Year of the Rat rather than to that of the Mouse. Of course there are examples in visual, oral and written culture in which the mouse is significant

The ascetic cat and mice in 'Arjuna's Penance', 7th century, from Mamallapuram, Tamil Nadu, India.

in its own right, and others in which the meaning of *mus* and *rattus* are one and the same, and need not apply solely to one genus or the other.

When we do see what we recognize clearly as impressions of mice, particularly in Japanese art of the Edo (1603–1868) and Meiji (1868–1912) periods, there is a real affection displayed for the animals that sits in stark contrast to most European representations of mice.

The mouse appears mostly in Asian art in religious iconography. Mice are depicted alongside two major household gods. Both are derived from Shiva, 'Auspicious One', the personification of destruction in the Trimurti or Hindu trinity along with Brahma and

Vishnu. The first is Shiva's son, Ganesha, the elephant-headed deity honoured by Hindus, Buddhists and Jains. The second is Daikoku, a Japanese god associated with the Buddhist Mahakala, a terrible form of Shiva. Daikoku's rodents are sometimes referred to as mice and sometimes as rats. The same can be said for Ganesha's mount, except that many put a case that it is instead a bandicoot rat (*Bandicota indica*),[1] with its large, rounded head, large, oval ears and short muzzle. The rodent's symbolism, however – if not its guise – is equally symptomatic of 'mouse'.

Asia is home to a stunning plethora of mice, many of which live in forests and deserts and are hardly ever seen. Those that are more familiar – mice of the *musculus domesticus* complex – cause a great deal of damage to crops and dwellings.[2] These include the Ryukyu mouse (*Mus caroli*) in East Asia, Nepal, Southeast Asia and Indonesia; and the fawn-coloured mouse (*M. cervicolor*) throughout South, Southeast and East Asia, and Indonesia. Both species live in rice fields, grassland and forests, and can be found around villages. Throughout Asia the most common house mice are *Mus musculus bactrianus* of the Indian subcontinent; *M. m. musculus* of Central Asia and China; *M. m. castaneus* of Southeast Asia; and *M. m. molossinus* of Japan. Japan is also home to the small and large Japanese field mouse (*Apodemus argentus* and *A. speciocus*), and, together with China and Korea, to the Korean field mouse (*A. peninsulae*). Other dominant mice include the spiny Cook's mouse (*M. cookii*), which presides in India, Nepal and Southeast Asia, and the Asiatic long-tailed tree mouse (*Vandeleuria oleracea*), which is native to South and Southeast Asia. The spiny field or flat-haired mouse (*M. platythrix*) lives only in India, throughout which it is common. Two of the smallest mouse species of India, the little Indian field mouse (*M. booduga*) and the earth-coloured mouse (*M. terricolor*), are also dominant, and exist in grass and cultivated fields.

A postcard of an elephant (rather calm, contrary to popular belief) with a mouse, 1921.

The mouse in India has been a problem for farmers, infesting rice and wheat fields, and towns and villages, since agriculture began around 9000 BC. During the monsoon mice take shelter in grain stores and in houses, where they contaminate food and

Roy Jamini,
Ganesha and
mouse *vahanas*,
c. 1943–4, ink
on paper.

spread disease. In Islam Allah's apostle is quoted in the Hadith of Bukhari (3:54, 3:55) as having described the mouse as one of five kinds of harmful animal that it is not a sin to kill, along with the crow, the kite, the scorpion and the rabid dog.[3] Manu, the first man of Hinduism, advises the kings not to select Mahidurga, a fort swarming with rats and mice, as their residence.[4] The mouse was a terrible pest in the Indus Valley. The people of Mohenjo-Daro, the civilization's largest settlement, built in 2600 BC, caught the rodents in specially designed terracotta traps. In ancient India the mouse was known as *vighna* or 'trouble'. It also shared its Sanskrit name, *mūsh*, with the word for 'thief'. The Laws of Manu (*c.* 200 BC–AD 200) warn pilferers of the corn that for their sinful acts they will be reborn as mice.[5] In the Vedas, the oldest Hindu scriptures, the mouse is given an almost demonic identity when it becomes the weapon of Yama, god of death, judge of the dead and lord of Kali-chi, the infernal regions.[6]

The mouse is also symbol of good luck in India. In the temple of Karni Mata at Deshok in Rajasthan, black rats are worshipped – believed to be the reincarnated souls of the goddess Karni Mata's devotees – yet the few white mice that live peacefully among them, are, for some unknown reason, held to be even more auspicious. (It is probably the case that their luckiness stems from the fact that they are rarely seen, like shooting stars.)

The Mouse is the vehicle of Ganesha, one of the panchayatana or five canonical gods of Hinduism, whose image exists in virtually every Indian home and is popular throughout Nepal. Its presence is also noted in what is now Pakistan, Tibet, Afghanistan

Worshipped mice and rats enjoying a drink of nourishing milk in the Karni Mata temple of Rajasthan, where they are held sacred, as the reincarnations of the goddess's devotees.

77

In Kawanabe Kyōsai's triptych *The Munificent Mice*, 1889, mice bring good fortune into the house of Daikoku.

and Central Asia, Sri Lanka, Myanmar, Thailand, Cambodia, Laos, Vietnam, Malaysia, Indonesia, Borneo and parts of the Pacific.[7] The mouse became associated with Ganesha in India, most Indologists agree, in around the eleventh or twelfth centuries AD, when it became the deity's *vahana*, or vehicle. For this, Ganesha is referred to as 'Mouse-Rider' in the Vedas, and is popularly depicted standing, sitting or dancing on the rodent. Ganesha's mouse is depicted in various sizes, from a tiny mouse dwarfed by the deity to one the size of a giant pig that Ganesha rides on in comfort. Ganesha is usually portrayed with his mouse in drawings, paintings, stone sculptures, pottery, bronze statues, advertisements and puppetry. Mice are often shown eating or stealing sweets piled up alongside him.

The mouse is thought to have already been connected to Shiva from Vedic times, when Rudra (a form of Shiva) is said to have had the mouse as his totem. Andrew Lang in *Custom and Myth* connects Rudra with the Mouse Apollo. He quotes the *Yajur-Veda* (1400–1000 BC): 'This portion belongs to thee O Rudra . . . whose animal is the mouse.'[8] Rudra is the 'Fierce One', who, like

Ganesha mounted on his mouse, Mushaka, in a Rajasthani watercolour of c. 1800.

his Greek counterpart and other gods of pestilence, is also a great healer.

The mouse is mentioned as Ganesha's mount in four of his eight incarnations in one of the religious texts dedicated to him, the Mudgala Purana (*c.* AD 1000–1500), in which the deity represents the overcoming of arrogance, confusion, greed and anger. The mouse here embodies wisdom and humility, but also the gluttony and wrath that Ganesha quashes beneath his feet. The mouse is also known for its mischievous behaviour. It is written in the Ganesha Purana (*c.* AD 1000–1500) that when Ganesha was a child, he caught a giant mouse that was tormenting his friends in his lasso, and made it his mount. The mouse was in fact a cursed celestial musician (*gandharva*), turned into a mouse by a sage as a punishment for walking over his feet. The Brahma-Vaivarta Purana (*c.* AD 1000) tells us that Vasundhara, the goddess of the earth, gave the mouse to Ganesha as a vehicle. The mouse, who swallows everything, is an apt vehicle for Ganesha, who holds the multiple universes in his belly. Ganesha is the god of wisdom, and the Remover of Obstacles (*Vighneshvara*); qualities we associate with the prophetic and all-penetrative mouse, capable of gnawing its way into or out of any space. According to the French Indologist Alain Daniélou in his book *The Myths and Gods of India*, the mouse is 'the all-pervading *atman* [soul] which lives in the hole called Intellect within every being'.[9]

Although an unlikely pair, the elephant and the mouse are both enemies of the farmer because they do a great deal of damage to corn. However, the mouse is presumed the destroyer to Ganesha's creator. It has been suggested that the mouse or rat signifies the lord of the harvest overcoming the pestilence of the field mouse.[10] We must not of course forget that the elephant, a symbol of the universe, is supposed to fear the mouse. A Tibetan myth attributes this fear to the rodent running inside the elephant's trunk and

Shibata Zeshin, *Mouse* (perhaps a rat?), *c.* 1870, lacquer on paper.

In this 17th-century Indian watercolour, a lady (Radha) complains to a companion about life in her husband's house; the cat and mouse scene above is a metaphor for the lady and her overbearing mother-in-law.

poisoning his brain.[11] According to a 2008 episode of Discovery TV's series *Mythbusters*, elephants are indeed afraid of mice, appearing genuinely startled on seeing one at close proximity.

A commentator on animals in the art of Nepal claims that the mouse is also relevant to Ganesha – sometimes given the appellation *Siddhidata*, 'the one who bestows success' – because he himself is such a successful being: omnivorous, adaptable and prolific, resourceful and unrelenting.[12] Although theft, with which the mouse is synonymous, is a sin in Hinduism (it is one of the seven vices or *vyasanas*), it can also be viewed positively. Daniélou writes that 'theft is the support of the immense being (*Brahma*)'.[13] Some Hindu divinities are known to steal or to steal back what is rightfully theirs – often objects to do with knowledge or fertility.

Krishna, as a child, is famous for stealing butter, a symbol of love. Stealing can be innocent and it can be important to divine power. Therefore the mouse is a useful tool to Ganesha, who can use him – a proficient thief and a creature of wisdom – to 'steal righteously' on his behalf, or at least to provide him with a constant food supply. The mouse is a sure sign of plentiful food, as he is to Daikoku; not only because where there is food there are mice, but because the mouse represents the will to survive.

Ganesha's mouse is called Mushaka, which comes from the Sanskrit for 'the stealthy one'. It pertains both to *mus* and to the Sanskrit word *mushká*, meaning testicle. Alice Getty in her book *Ganeśa* (1936) describes the god's mouse or rat as a phallic symbol. When the god is shown sitting sideways on Mushaka, the rodent resembles a lingam or phallus, representing both the fertility of the earth and sexual desire, over which Ganesha has great power. In Tibetan mythology a blue Mushaka spews forth gems at Rakta Ganapati's (Ganesha's) feet. Jewels, honey, milk, nectar and semen appear in myth and art as metaphors for previous fertility. Jewels must also act as a metaphor for valuable, fertile grain. In areas of Bengal that is the meaning of the mouse-earth with which a Bengali daughter repays her mother for giving her life and caring for her. In this part of rural Bengal the mouse is associated with Lakshmi, goddess of light, wisdom, prosperity and the harvest. The mouse's association with penetration and holes or burrows made it a symbol of genitalia in Hindu myth. An Orissan myth tells us that when women had no sexual organs, it was the rat that made the first opening. In a myth of Indra the god is branded with 1,000 eyes that turn into vaginas and are referred to as 'mice'. (A folktale from Korea presents the vagina as a harmful beast, and the mouse as a filthy, furry devourer, when a mouse accidentally creeps into a woman's vagina and bites her lover's penis.) In a myth of Shiva a mouse becomes a penetrative trickster with whom the god gains forced entry both to the house and the goddess. Having been tricked by Parvati, Shiva takes revenge by turning himself into a mouse to chew through the goddess's bodice. He then appears in the guise of an old and undesirable tailor who sews it back up, but refuses to leave until she has allowed him to make love to her.

The burrowing nature of the mouse is also drawn upon in the Vedas. The mouse appears as a sacrificial offering of Shiva in the Yajurveda, buried beneath the ground while Brahmin priests practice 'rituals for the fulfilment of desire'.[14] In another myth Agni, the god of fire, hides from the other gods by transforming himself into a mouse and burrowing underground.

While the mouse is connected to gods and Brahmins, there are also some animal folktales of India in which the mouse represents Untouchable (*dalit*) castes. Two stories are dedicated to the mouse in the *Panchatantra*, a celebrated collection of ancient Indian animal fables compiled in the third century BC. One, also familiar from Aesop, tells of mice who free elephants from snares. The other uses the mouse as a symbol of low-caste people to teach that the low castes should marry among each other. The story describes a mouse that falls from a vulture's beak into the hands of a sage. The sage changes the mouse into a maiden, brings her up as his daughter and, when she reaches the age of twelve, tries to arrange her marriage. The maiden rejects the marriage of the sun, the wind and the mountain, but when she finds a mouse, she realizes that she is of the same kind, and wishes to be changed back into a mouse to marry him. There are similar stories in which animal brides are human but wear mouse-skin coats that can be taken off and put on at will, enabling them to shift between human and animal form. Ultimately of course the girl becomes permanently human, as marriage ensures her purity and acceptance into society. Mice seem to be useful animals for thinking

Tangore glass painting, featuring Ganesha.

about transitions and rites of passage, probably because as the smallest animals, they represent beginnings. In the Hitopadesha (AD 800–850), a famous collection of Indian stories, when a mouse again falls from a vulture's beak into the hands of a sage, he turns it into a cat to stop it from being eaten; then into a dog, and then a tiger, until he reads its mind, finds it is thinking about eating him, and changes it back into a mouse again.

Tales of mouse weddings are prolific throughout Asia. They are popularised through folktale, folkart and ritual. The early twentieth-century anthropologist James G. Frazer relates in *The Golden Bough* (1922) how in Indonesia, after Friday Mosque, four pairs of mice are married, and each pair is pushed out to sea in a foot-long boat filled with rice and fruit.[15] Chinese opera tells stories of arranged marriages in which mice marry cats and are then eaten. Similar anthropomorphic stories are typical of Japanese

Tsukioka Yoshitoshi's satirical rendering of *The Battle of the Cats and the Mice*, 1859, woodblock print, ink and colour on paper.

Shibata Zeshin, *Mice*, c. 1890, woodblock print.

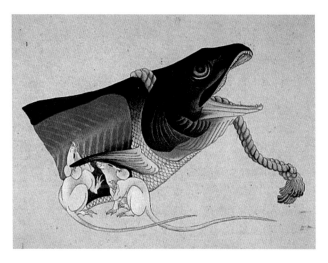

A fashionable woman wearing a costume embossed with mice eating peppers in a woodblock print c. 1820 by Keisai Eisen. Other examples of mice and women in art from the 19th century include those in which mice crawl up the clothes of seated women.

Katsushika Hokusai (1760–1849), mice eating a salmon, as a representation of famine; from an album of paintings.

scroll paintings from the Kamakura (1185–1333), Muromachi (1336–1573) and Edo (1603–1868) periods, often involving a marriage between a mouse and a human. Images of married mice can serve to charm rodents, like newly-weds, out of the family home. At Chinese New Year, in the province of Shandong, parents tell their children that the mice of the house are getting married and that if they go to bed early and close their eyes they will be able to hear the wedding march.[16] Wedding gifts are left for the mice by some families in the form of rice and sweets. Prints and scissor paper-cut images of the wedding procession have become a decorative feature at traditional rural weddings in the province.

The relationship between mice and fertility/new life must account for the use of mice in Chinese and Korean traditional medicine, in which baby mice continue to be stewed, at first live, in rice wine for up to a year; the wine is then used to heal a variety of ailments. Mice have been used, along with a menagerie of other animals, in folk medicine throughout Asia for thousands of

years, often as an aphrodisiac. They are mentioned for their reme-
dial purposes a great deal in medieval Graeco-Islamic medicine
(including the medicine of the Prophet, *tibb al-nabawi*), which
drew heavily on zootherapy.

The mouse's most significant role in East Asian culture is as the
totem animal of the household god Daikoku, with whom the
mouse is represented on wood- and paper-cuts and in fan and
scroll paintings, ink drawings, statues, lanterns and greetings
cards. Daikoku is a household god in Japan but is also worshipped
in China and Tibet. He is popularly shown with rice bales surrounded by mice and gold coins (*ryō*). With each strike of his
money mallet, Daikoku – who is invoked by merchants to incite
trade – is said to bring riches to the land. Daikoku is frequently
shown surrounded by white mice, or with one large white mouse
– the size of a large dog – sitting or sitting upright, sometimes
robed. White mice in China are considered particularly lucky
symbols. Chinese priests used albino mice in auguries, which
may have had something to do with Daikoku, who at one time
was associated with magic and necromancy. Sometimes images
of Daikoku's mice – like many of the classic Chinese and Japanese
renderings of mice with melons and eggs, as symbols of fertility
– are attributed to the rat, but could easily be of larger mouse
species, such as large Japanese field mice.

Generally speaking the Chinese and Japanese connect both
mice and rats with fertility and prosperity. Traditionally they
credit both for the introduction of rice. This association, and
the positive renderings of mice in art and religious iconography, may be connected to the fact that mouse plagues have not
been so catastrophic or occurred as frequently in China and
Japan as elsewhere in the world.

The Japanese do not always make a clear distinction between
the rat and mouse, typically using one word, *nezumi*, to signify

みがての みずね

RRR

both. In some texts the word *norako* is used to denote the mouse, or, in others, reflecting modern Japanese, *hatsuka-nezumi*, which is used to talk specifically about the mouse as a 'small rat'. Clearly the mouse is defined by the rat in Japanese culture, rather than the other way around. The Chinese give preference to the rat (*da shu*, 'big mouse') over the mouse (*shu*) in their zodiac. Therefore most 'mice' in Chinese art and symbolism should be taken as rats unless stated otherwise. In Tibetan astrology the *byi-ba* (which can refer to both mouse and rat) is one of the twelve year signs. Translators typically prefer to translate *byi-ba* as 'mouse'.

During the Edo period in Japan, specifically the Meiwa Era (1764–71), breeding interesting colours of *nezumi* was particularly popular in Osaka. In the aforementioned *Yoso-tama-no-kakehashi*, or 'a bridge to obtaining novel jewel-like *nezumi*' (1775), the mouse is introduced as a breed of rat. It is described as 'being small, having a rabbit-like body shape with a hairless tail. Its coat colour is dark grey, its whiskers are long, and its eyes pop out.'[17] The growing aesthetic interest in mice and rats perhaps had something to do with the beautiful art of the eighteenth and nineteenth centuries, in which mice become individual subjects in delicate, stylized paintings such as Shibata Zeshin's untitled lacquer on paper. In other paintings the rodents are portrayed as charming, inquisitive, playful, whimsical figures, frolicking with each other, rolling on their backs and becoming a source of entertainment for men or gods.

Mice in Japanese New Year's greetings cards through the twentieth century are reflective of modern artistic movements in the West, with some examples becoming particularly abstract. One illustration from a children's storybook from the 1930s presents a mouse composed of Art Deco geometric shapes. Mice have, characteristically, kept up with the times. Today in India, Mushaka alongside Ganesha is popular in animated films with religious themes like *Bal Ganesh* (dir. Pankaj Sharma, 2007), and in Japan we find the mouse, including futuristic mouse-like icon Pikachu, in anime, manga and video games.

The mouse in Asia is as contradictory as ever, representing both good luck and bad. Largely it is an auspicious animal, a divine being with as many virtues as vices, a creature of perception, prosperity and pleasure. Physically the mouse can be miniscule or gargantuan, fawn-coloured or royal blue, naked or clothed like an emperor. The mouse is a key figure in the ancient and modern religious iconography of two major Asian household gods, and as such is more relevant in Asia today as a cultural-religious symbol than anywhere else in the world. Together with these gods, the mouse functions as a sign of wealth – no more than a gold coin or a grain of rice – but equally as a complex and comic character with a history and an identity of its own. The mouse in Asia is divine, dirty, vulnerable, beautiful and wise; a creature of high and low status, possessing qualities we want to both harness and suppress.

4 The Mouse in the Indigenous Cultures of the Americas

While history and archaeology have not produced the same spectacular stories of mouse plagues in the Pre-Colombian Americas as in the classical world, the inclusion of mice and rats in allegories of war between tribes, kings and conquistadores points to a strong association between the rodents and destruction. Either a literal or metaphorical invasion would have inspired the sudden appearance of mice and rats in the pottery of the Peruvian Middle Nazca (AD 450–550), for example, where armies of highly stylized rodents are painted on vases, bowls and other, probably ceremonial, receptacles.

Mice appear more as negative symbols in the powerful agricultural civilizations of Mesoamerica and the Andes, where they destroyed staple foods that had come to develop divine economic status, such as maize, the corn from which the first Mesoamericans believed themselves to have been born. The eleventh book of the Florentine Codex, a sixteenth-century ethnographic study of Mesoamerica, describes how the mouse eats like a human, seeking out maize as well as other precious commodities such as chilli, chocolate, cacao beans and the roots of the maguey plant, noting how the mouse 'gnaws all'.[1] It was probably for this reason that the superstitious Aztecs considered the mouse, or *quimichin* in the Náhuatl language, a bad omen, especially when it entered the home. Mice were also known to the

Maya for eating the ramón plant, an important tree in the Yucatan that had edible nutritious fruit. The most blameworthy mouse was the prolific spiny pocket mouse (*Chaetodipus spinatus*) or *xpukil ch'o'*, a rodent apparently capable of eating 150 per cent of its body weight in fruit in one sitting.[2]

The most pestilent mice to the Aztecs would have been two species of deer mouse, the white-footed mouse (*Peromyscus leucopus*) and the Aztec mouse (*P. aztecus*). The mice of Latin America are diverse, predominantly composed of species of deer mice (*Peromyscus*), pocket mice (Heteromyidae), Oldfield mice (*Thomasomys*), grass mice (*Akodon/Abrothrix*), climbing mice (*Rhipidomys*) and leaf-eared mice (*Graomys/Phyllotis*). The variety is rich and unique. The native mice of the Americas are New World Cricetidae rodents, classified in the murid subfamily Sigmodontinae. They can be distinguished from their European cousins by their white underbellies and bicoloured tails, dark

Mouse Woman Panel by Haida artist Jay Simeon, 2011, red cedar.

above and light below. The Cricetidae are thought to have island-hopped from Central to South America across the Panama land bridge sometime during the Pliocene (5.3–2.6 MYA).[3] *Mus musculus* has more recently become the most destructive mouse in the Americas since it arrived with Europeans in the sixteenth century.

There is some evidence to suggest that some later Meso-american Indians worshipped the mouse as a form of pacification. In Jalisco, Mexico, a stuffed mouse was kept in a local temple in a place called Ratontita or 'Place of the Mouse/Rat', and was found by anthropologists in the late nineteenth century.[4]

The Maya (*c.* 2000 BC–AD 1700) had for centuries before kept boa constrictors in the roofs of their homes to catch mice.[5] In Mayan and later Mesoamerican art the mouse and its serpent predator represent the constant cycle of death and rebirth, which in these parts of the Americas was intrinsically linked to constant war and conquest, to bloodthirsty sacrificial ritual and to the immortality of all-powerful kings. The mouse and snake possessed potent connotations of the sacrificed and the sacrifice, the defeated and the successor, the slave and the empire,

'Meadow jumping mouse (*Zapus hudsonius americanus*)', in an illustration from Audubon's *Viviparous Quadrupeds of North America* (1845–54).

and the lower class and the royal lineage, of which the serpent was a powerful symbol.

The Aztecs also associated the mouse literally with the destructive forces of the female stellar deities, or 'demons', Tzitzimime. In the Aztec calendar the end of each 52-year cycle was marked with a New Fire Ceremony, which involved human sacrifice and the putting out of old fires and lighting of new ones. This was carried out to prevent the Tzitzimime from 'devouring' the earth.[6] It was believed that the moon's eclipse a few days before the ceremony could bring about miscarriage in a pregnant woman or turn the foetus into a mouse.[7] Various accounts also note that children were pinched to keep them awake for fear that they would turn into grain-eating mice.[8] It is possible that mice were connected to the end of the world because they appeared in large numbers after recurring droughts or cyclical ecological phenomena, bringing great famine and disease.

The Aztecs used the mouse, a symbol of death, in funerary art. A large sculpted mouse or rat can be found in a stone box containing the ashes of the Ahuitzotl who ruled over Aztec Tenochtitlan between 1486 and 1481, the father and predecessor of Montezuma II. In other parts of Pre-Colombian South America the mouse has been connected archeologically to death and the afterlife. The rodent appears in the pottery of the Peruvian Moche (AD 100–700), which was typically adorned with gods, warriors, sacrificers, impersonators and shamans. It was a widespread Pan-Mesoamerican belief that the bat – the messenger of the dead and symbol of reincarnation – was a transformed mouse, rat or shrew. There is an old story about mice who, envious of bats' ability to fly, jumped over a canyon to be rewarded by the Creator with a pair of wings. The mice that afterwards made it across were all transformed into bats.

A mouse and a 'merchant–spy', from the Florentine Codex, a 16th-century ethnographic study of the Aztec world by the Spanish friar Bernadino de Sahagún.

The idea of mice as chrysalises metamorphosing into the eternal winged soul seems like a promise of immortality to tribes at war, especially as plagues of mice are so often metaphors for armies.

The Aztecs also used mice in medicine. Because of the rodent's relationship to the night, the mice, along with other nocturnal animals such as the wolf, were used in medicine for epilepsy, which was, it was believed, controlled by the moon's phases. Sufferers were apparently fumigated with the odour of a mouse's nest heated on coals.[9]

The Aztecs also used the word for 'mouse' as a metaphor for *nahualoztomeca*, the spies who brought information on new sources of wealth to their emperors. Like the spy, the mouse is described in the Florentine Codex as often passing unnoticed, hunting out precious things, no matter how inaccessible.[10] The nocturnal mouse was a suitable animal for this role, since the Aztecs connected the night with invisibility, trickery and evil. The Codex similarly notes how 'mouse' was a synonym for 'eavesdropper',[11] like a fly on the wall.

While the agricultural civilizations of Meso- and South America associated the destructive mouse with famine, in some foraging and hunting societies of North America the mouse was instead a symbol of *plentiful* food because of its unrelenting resourcefulness. The Siuoan Hidatsa people of North Dakota, for

Greedy mice in the Florentine Codex.

example, were recorded in the 1930s by anthropologist A. W. Bowers as using physical representations of mice as totems and good-luck talismans. Bowers notes how the people prayed to a stuffed mouse for food; the leader tied the mouse in his hair whenever he went to hunt.[12] The mouse represents a perpetual source of sustenance, both in real terms, because it almost never goes hungry; and metaphorically, because as the ultimate prey animal, the mouse underpins the food chain.

Where they appear in stories and art, mice are often depicted together with a predator, denoting the 'circle of life': the owl, the eagle, the fox, the coyote and the snake. With these animals the mouse enacts other power struggles between tribes and sexes. In a number of oral tales, many of which have been told and reshaped over centuries, the mouse, as we find all over the world, is often a popular figure – wise, courageous and victorious against greater beings.

In reality, prior to European colonization, there is no doubt that the mouse caused chaos among agricultural societies, since the farming of wheat and maize began as far back as 7,000 years ago, east of the Mississippi. Post-colonization, places named after mice in North America, such as the town Souris (Fr. 'mouse') in Manitoba, Canada, and its Souris River, which interestingly meanders through Missouri, may well suggest recurring plagues in those areas. The most invasive murine animals in North America are the widespread deer mice (*Peromyscus maniculatus*) and introduced house mouse, the black rat (*Rattus norvegicus*) and the brown (*R. rattus*); and it is probably to these rodents that we can attribute infestations in settlements like that of the Cahto of the Round Valley Reservation in California, where the people were forced to rebuild their homes every two years as a vermin control measure during the nineteenth century.[13] Other North American mice include sub-species of groove-toothed harvest mice (*Reithrodontomys*, *Cricetidae*) and pygmy mice (*Baiomyini*, *Cricetidae*), jumping mice (*Zapodinae*, *Dipodidae*) and pocket mice (*Perognathus*, *Heteromyidae*). Jumping mice, such as the meadow jumping mouse (*Zapus hudsonius*) and the western jumping mouse (*Z. princeps*), are common in the deserts and plains of North America.

The mouse appears in a number of creation stories as the first mammal on earth. The Ia'tik people of the Western Pueblos of Arizona tell a story about human twin sisters who are born beneath the earth and bring pictures of animals to life, and when they emerge into the upper world they sing a song to create the mouse. Once they have created it they send it forth to reproduce, and the Earth Mother shows the sisters how to catch and eat a mouse.

The idea of the mouse as the first animal to be born and the first to die (and the first to be reborn) can be found in stories from northernmost tribes about mice and their predators. In some myths of the Bering Sea – which lies between Alaska and Siberia – the owl, having eaten a mouse, excretes it before then defecating the bones of a number of other animals that return to life, filling the land and sea with game.

Most North American mouse stories derive from the peoples of the far north, including those of the northwest Pacific coast, who connect the mouse with the soul, the underworld, magic and the moon. The Haida tribe of the Queen Charlotte Islands depicts mice and ermines in storytelling as guides to the nether regions (both are burrowing creatures). They tell stories about Mouse Woman, who offers guidance to those between worlds: a secondary but nonetheless prominent figure pictured on totem poles and in traditional art. Mouse Woman is known to save the dying by sending pieces of copper to the underworld as substitutes for the dead. In the story of Asdiwal

– a tale recorded by the American anthropologist Claude Lévi-Strauss in the 1960s – Mouse Woman takes the protagonist on a subterranean journey, during which he meets the walruses he had hunted and must cure in order to return to earth. The Haida also imagined the mouse as prophetic, using a form of myomancy in which the rodents' ear movements provided answers to vital questions. They believe that their people learned magic from a mouse disguised as a beautiful woman. Together with the neighbouring Tlingit, they tell stories of mice entering the bodies of the dead as disease-causing spirits, probably because the mouse is a common sight around carrion. The Tlingit consider the spirit of the mouse the strongest of all the animal spirits, and depict the rodent, alongside the rat and the mink, on the costumes of mystics and medicine people.[14] The association between mice and witchcraft may be born out of a shared relationship to antisocial behaviour, with mice and witches both guilty of stealing.[15]

Mouse worship can also be found in this part of the world. The Dene, a tribe of Arctic and Subarctic Canada, worshipped a 'yellow mouse with a pointed snout' well into the nineteenth century. They believed that a leaping mouse would cause the

Preble's meadow jumping mouse (*Zapus hudsonius preblei*).

moon's eclipse, and that they themselves would 'return' to the moon after death.[16] The strong association between the mouse and lunar symbolism in this part of the Americas no doubt had its origins in Central Asia, from where the ancestors of many northern tribes migrated across the Bering Strait between 1200 BC and 800 BC, and then again in the thirteenth century AD.

The ancestors of the Dene – who originated in Xi-Xia, a Uighur Turkish Kingdom – were known as the Yuezhi 'moon clan'. They were the contemporaries of the horse-riding Iranian Scythians who are said to have worshipped the Apollo *Smintheus*, the Mouse Apollo, and worn the skins of mice in his honour. The Yuezhi founded the Kushan Empire in the former Greek Bactria (present-day northern Afghanistan) in the first century AD. They are considered the ancestors of the North American Yuchi of the southeast, who, together with the Cherokee tribe, into which they were later absorbed, named many of their places after mice. An association with the underworld may also be attributed to the eastern Slavs (of what is now Russia, Ukraine and Belarus) who fled to North America under Mongol invasion in the thirteenth century. Echoing the beliefs of ancient Greece, they were said to have termed the Milky Way the 'Mouse Way' or 'Mouse Path', identifying it as the route taken by the soul to the underworld.[17]

Irrespective of this, the brown burrowing mouse would seem to travel between worlds, emerging from the whiteness of the snow and darting back in at the sight of a fox or an owl. Alaska and its neighbouring territories are home to deer mice and jumping mice, as well as a vast number of shrews and lemmings, and countless species of voles (including the tundra vole, *Microtus oeconomus*, of the Arctic), which can behave and appear like mice. White mice are thought by the Inuit of the Arctic to fall from clouds in snowstorms. These 'mice' are in fact northern collared lemmings (*Dicrostonyx groenlandicus*), the only species in the mouse family to change the colour of its fur in the winter, from brown to pure white.

In cold regions rodents are particularly destructive when they eat into winter supplies and grease boxes. An oil receptacle belonging to the Haida is adorned with two mice at each end – probably northwestern deer mice (*Peromyscus keeni*), known to enter homes in winter – crawling inwards, representing the animal's fondness for grease.[18] Despite the mouse's status as vermin, many clans traditionally acknowledge its powers in their myths and adopt its image as part of their ceremonial and martial dress. The Tlingit wore warrior helmets carved in the shape of a mouse's face from as early as the eighteenth century, and the Kwakwaka'waka of Northern Vancouver Island use mouse masks in celebratory dances. As the ultimate prey the mouse is an unusual choice for martial dress. However, it appears as a warrior figure in stories from across America, often as the surprising victor over much greater beings. In the Blackfoot tale from Montana 'Why Blackfeet Never Kill Mice', a mouse is elected as chief but gives away his new-found superior position to man, since he is too small and not warrior-like enough.

The mouse is sometimes depicted in the stories of northern hunting peoples as having comic battles with the raven, with which rodents compete for animal carcasses in reality and myth. In a myth from the Siberian Arctic some sadistic mice take revenge on a raven for stealing their food by stitching red fur to its eyebrows to make it think its house is on fire, and sewing a bladder-bag to its buttocks so that it cannot find its droppings and is frightened to hear them rattling around. The Siberian Inuit believe in giant fish, giant birds, giant shrews and giant mice. The American anthropologist Franz Boas (1858–1942), in his studies of far northern tribes in Canada, writes about the father of Sedna, who rules over the depths of the sea – an underworld – in the myths of Baffin Island. This man, a dwarf apparently no larger than a man's finger, possesses the strength of a giant and pulls a sledge of mice, and sometimes appears as a mouse himself.[19] Some stories also tell of sea shrews that drill holes through seal-skin kayaks with their pointed snouts, before tunnelling through the bodies of the ill-fated occupants.

In other parts of North America the common motif of mice gnawing through boats appears in the stories of a number of tribes, including the Koruk of California, in whose tale the mouse is a hero for sinking the boats of the enemy. Largely, however, the mouse is credited as a healer, capable on occasion of bringing other, 'greater' animals back from the dead. In a story from Idaho, a shamanistic mouse referred to as the Sly One brings a salmon killed by a rattlesnake back to life by rubbing the fish bones together for days with salmon oil.

In a folktale from the Great Plains commonly referenced in anthologies of Native American myths and legends, the 'Story of Jumping Mouse', the mouse is integral to the healing process, representing a state of sickness and spiritual ignorance preceding the attainment of immortality. The story tells of a young mouse that goes on a pilgrimage to the Great Medicine Lake. Along the way it selflessly sacrifices both of its eyes to a needy buffalo and wolf. When the mouse reaches the lake its sight is miraculously restored. A frog encourages it to jump as high as it can to try to catch a glimpse of the sacred lake, before transforming the leaping rodent into an eagle. The story alludes to the pilgrimages to sacred mountains on which men go to collect medicine, undergoing a series of visions. It might to some extent reflect a mythic theme that looks ahead to a time when great heroes will return to their people with powerful medicine to

American deer mouse.

restore former glory. The mouse may not be a symbol of immortality per se, but plays a vital role in representations of its attainment.

The mouse appears as a symbol of healing, along with the eagle, bear and buffalo, in Native American 'medicine wheels', honoured, in their varying forms and sizes, by most Indian nations as healing tools as well as signs of peace. In various New Age texts on Native American spirituality, the mouse in the medicine wheel, as the 'spirit-keeper' of the south, symbolizes the sun, childhood and the Asian race. 'Mouse people' are described as having various positive qualities, including being organized, intrepid and tolerant.

The mouse in the ancient and modern indigenous cultures of the Americas is an important symbol of new life and death, and as such has been implicated in various ways and among various people in ideas of the natural and cosmic order, spiritually; and in notions of power, socially and politically. In the cultures of North America the mouse plays a largely positive role, existing in what is still very much part of a living religion. The mouse is a friend, offering guidance, bringing food and medicine to the needy, selflessly sacrificing itself for the greater good, helping people across rivers, retrieving lost or stolen items and biting holes in the boats of the enemy. Further back in history, Pre-Colombian civilizations associated the mouse more with fear; fear of death, conquest and the end of the world. Yet the meanings of the mouse cannot be divided between north and south, and good and evil, especially across such periods of time. As is always the case with the mouse, it is eternally both positive and negative. While it is destructive, it appears that we can learn a lot from its will to survive and achieve, as a creature with endless enemies that strives to attain a higher sense of being. The mouse is transformed into an eagle or bat in imaginings of the great and never-ending, self-sacrificing quest for immortality.

5 The Mouse in Art, Film and Literature

The mouse, more than any other animal, has evolved in art. Some examples of the 'postmodern mouse', in their hyperreal, technological forms, are hardly recognizable from mice in art even half a century ago. So what do we think of when we consider the mouse in visual culture? Probably not the Renaissance *still-leven* or still-lifes of the Dutch and Flemish schools in which the mouse enjoyed a good deal of fame, or infamy, in the seventeenth century; hidden among fruit, flowers, seafood and game, reminding us of the brevity of life and the futility of earthly goods. Instead we naturally call to mind images of mice from our lifetimes; images from American popular culture rather than European art, and no doubt of one mouse in particular: a hero of the twentieth century that has become one of the most recognized images in the world. Mickey Mouse and other on-screen murine heroes seem to speak, in contrast to their simulacral ancestors, of promise, prosperity, utopias and even immortality. So how and why has the use of the mouse in the visual arts changed so much, and what does it mean?

In the early sixteenth century, Michelangelo intended, although he didn't actually get around to it, to carve a mouse on a monument to the Renaissance ruler of Florence, Giuliano de' Medici, to signify 'the oblivion of time in opposition to enduring fame'.[1] The mouse, as Herbert Friedmann describes in his

Gerrit Dou and Nicolaas Verkolje, *The Mouse Trap*, c. 1690–1715, mezzotint.

Bestiary for Saint Jerome (1980), is 'the great devourer', gnawing everything in its wake, 'representing the destructive nature of time and the transience of human existence'.[2]

In the early Renaissance, the mouse's avaricious appetite still resonated with medieval depictions of hell as the open mouth of a monster, and with Satan as a multi-mouthed devourer; the rodent's gnawing was identified with sin and judgement. A bestiary from Oxford's Bodleian Library likens the mouse to 'greedy men that make the goods of others their prey'.[3] Tales from popular

A mouse hides in Abraham van Beyeren's *Banquet Still-life with a Mouse*, 1667, oil on canvas.

folklore told of mice that ate men alive, often as vengeance for the mistreatment of the underclasses, of which the rodents are so commonly symbolic. Mice were said to have eaten whole powerful leaders at banquets, and sailed on ships (in one particular tale, in the carcasses of pomegranates, symbols of the Resurrection and the blood of martyrs), devouring the men on board. The Italian naturalist Ulisse Aldrovandi (1522–1605) wrote of King Popelus II, who, having murdered his uncles, was gnawed to death by their souls in the form of mice. A story catalogued by Sabine Baring-Gould in his *Curious Myths of the Middle Ages* (1866) relays how Bishop Hatto of Mainz was

Niccolò Colantonio, *St Jerome and the Lion*, c. 1445, oil on panel.

attacked and eaten in his tower by mice and rats possessed by
the souls of the dead, for burning his townspeople alive during
the plague year 970. Mice abounded in late-medieval depictions of the Black Death, recalling biblical pestilence, a form of
divine punishment. As Otto Neustratter identifies in his essay
'Mice in Plague Pictures', however, the rodents function merely
as signs of and omens for death, rather than as the cause of
the epidemic.[4]

Henry Marsh,
*Bishop Hatto and
the Rats*, c. 1866–7,
wood engraving.

Plague of Ashod, in a detail from the 'Morgan Bible', 1240s.

Death of Eli and
Plague of Mice.

Between the fifteenth and eighteenth centuries, artists from Italy, Germany and the Low Countries drew upon the mouse as a symbol of death, evil and judgement. Together with the fly and the worm, the mouse became an important part of the iconography of the memento mori genre, which expounded the Latin phrase 'remember your morality'; an idea that Christians of the period were encouraged to reflect upon almost constantly. These works highlighted the emptiness of earthly goods – of beauty, pleasure and power – in light of the prospect of hell. In the Italian art of the period the mouse appears alongside divine figures of virtue with saints or shepherds; while in works from Northern Europe the rodent is scarcely pictured with men, finding itself instead amid objects of nature, hiding like a demon in paradise in bountiful, cornucopian still-lifes.

Friedmann draws our attention to an early Renaissance painting by the Neapolitan artist Niccolò Colantonio entitled *St Jerome and the Lion* (*c.* 1445), in which a tiny mouse in the bottom right-hand corner gnaws at some papers while the saint removes thorns from a lion's paw. Although concealed, as mice so often are in art, the furtive mouse plays, as it always does, as much of an important role in this allegorical work about the overcoming of evil as do its main subjects. The mouse's obliteration of papers (which we assume to be ancient literature or historical works), together with the hourglass on the left-hand side, are natural and man-made reminders of the destructive nature of time. They seem to connote the certain death and judgement of even the most pious or celebrated of men and beasts. As well as referencing time, the obliterated papers also reference the Humanist belief in the relationship between scholarship and transcendance to the after-life. Humanism, as a religious and educational movement, gave prominence to human knowledge, seeing it as a reflection of the divine. It also taught that everything in creation is a symbol of God, and that God can be found in the individual human soul.

Ulisse Aldrovandi, *Cat on a Ledge with Mouse and Fruit*, c. 1580, oil on canvas.

The painting thus seems to promote education as a means of acquiring godliness.

The mouse appeared with saints throughout Europe, in art and literature, as a sign of malevolence. The rodents were pictured in ecclesiastical decoration and illuminated manuscripts in France, Germany and the Netherlands, running up the cloak, crosier or pastoral staff of plague saint Gertrude of Nivelles (*c.* 626–659), the patron saint of suriphobia or the fear of mice, to whom the rodents were thought to spend the first night after their deaths as symbols of souls in purgatory. St Gertrude, who received gold and silver mice at her shrine in Cologne as late as 1822, was prayed to for protection against field mice. In some bloodthirsty texts the mice eat her heart. St Fina of San Gimignano (1238–1253) was also plagued by mice that are said to have gnawed at her sores as she lay dying. An early fifteenth-century tabernacle by the Italian painter Lorenzo di Niccolò, depicting scenes from the saint's life, show St Fina's mother beating hordes of mice off her daughter's bed while the Devil tries to throw her down the stairs.

Robert Campin, St Joseph building a mousetrap in his workshop, in a detail of the right panel of the *Annunciation Triptych*, c. 1425.

Jacopo Ligozzi
(c. 1547–c. 1632),
drawing of a
garden dormouse
and mole.

Around the same time, in the Netherlands, the painter Robert Campin acknowledged the evil of the mouse in his *Annunciation Triptych*, in which St Joseph drills mousetraps in his workshop. The mousetrap is a metaphor for the Holy Cross, which St Augustine of Hippo (AD 354–430) had described centuries before as Christ's bait with which to capture the Devil.[5] In the late fifteenth and early sixteenth centuries the artists Jacopo Ligozzi, Jan van Os and Georg Flegel, in Italy, the Netherlands and Germany respectively, all showed mice cracking open walnuts in still-lifes as transience motifs and symbols of Christ's body, inferring the inevitability of death and universality of evil. Jan van Os depicts what is clearly a garden dormouse (when we would imagine him to picture the more notorious house or field mouse), perhaps because of its more interesting fur-covered tail and mask-like facial markings.

In seventeenth-century Italy the Baroque painter Guercino portrayed two young shepherds gazing at a mouse and a fly loitering on a human skull in an exuberant depiction of Arcadia. The painting, *Et in Arcadia ego* (1618), is a reminder that death

Guercino,
*Et in Arcadia
ego*, 1618–22,
oil on canvas.

exists everywhere, even in the most idyllic and heavenly of worlds, and that nobody, not even shepherds – custodians of life itself – are immune from it.

We know by now that the mouse is almost never depicted alone in art, instead finding its meaning in the context of other forms. In a beautiful print by the Dutch engraver Cornelis Visscher, *The Large Cat* (1657), a malevolent-looking mouse creeps up behind a large, noble tabby that is sleeping peacefully. When portrayed alongside the mouse, the cat was sometimes used as a Christ metaphor in Renaissance art, often with cross marks on its back, echoing themes of folktales in which the cat is the protector against the Devil, who disguises himself as a mouse in order to enter heaven or the ark. Interestingly, in contrast to most cat-and-mouse works of art, which usually play on monarchy–republic power struggles, in Visscher's piece it

is not the cat that is the potential danger, but its prey. A figure that is barely seen at first, the mouse is a reminder of the lurking evil that is always there – the greed, the temptation, the iniquity – that catches us when we least expect it.

However, when pictured with the cat, the mouse is also a useful subject for portraying the persecuted, in religious as well as political contexts. In an earlier engraving by Albrecht Dürer depicting *The Fall of Man* (1504), a mouse pictured beneath Adam represents his vulnerability to the sin of Eve, which is embodied in the cat at her feet. Eve is also accompanied by the serpent, and Adam by the pure symbol of the parrot. An ox in the background, a Christ symbol, watches the inevitability of the scene.

Visscher also printed *The Mousetrap* (c. 1650), an engraving in which a young boy and girl stand side by side; the boy holds a candle and the girl a cage containing a mouse. Artists after him during the seventeenth century depicted similar nocturnal

scenes in which candles and mousetraps seem to allude to male and female sexual organs. A mezzotint by Dutch artist Nicolaas Verkolje portrays a nocturnal scene in which a smiling, seated woman with a large, empty bowl at her waist appears to be educating a young, curious man; she holds a mousetrap in one hand and a candle in the other as he leans towards her, pointing at the device. The French engraver Claude Mellan produced an erotic, allegorical engraving on the same theme, *La Sourcière*. The mousetrap itself plays only a small physical role, but a defining metaphorical one, in the complex composition, which is dominated by three boys lying between the open legs of a provocative, reclining, naked woman on a bed.

The mousetrap is an obvious symbol of the female pudendum, a sort of *vagina dentata*. By default the mouse is then the phallus, and we see countless scenes in satirical art for the centuries that follow in which women are traumatized by the mouse as an aggressive phallic symbol, wholly defined by its naked tail. Still, mice are also often imagined as feminine creatures,

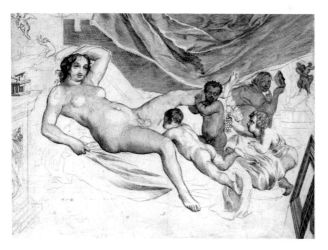

timid and themselves vulnerable: the female, perhaps, to the male rat. They are associated more with female sexuality, largely because of their shared negative associations in the Christian imagination.

In the sixteenth century the Italian writer Alciati wrote of the mouse as 'effeminate and promiscuous', an animal of 'sexual pleasure and voluptuousness'. The mouse became a popular metaphor for the female lover between the fifteenth and eighteenth centuries. In *Romeo and Juliet* (*c.* 1597) Lady Capulet refers to her husband as a 'mouse-hunt' to indicate his womanizing ways, and in *Hamlet* (*c.* 1600) the protagonist pronounces to Gertrude: 'Let the blowt king temp't you againe to bed / Pinch wanton on your cheek, call you his mouse.' Erasmus (1466–1536) described white mice as particularly lecherous in his book of adages, *Adagia*.

White fancy mice appear centuries later as metaphors for the passive female in Wilkie Collins's Gothic novel *The Woman in White* (1859), darting in and out of the villainous Count Fosco's

Aubrey Beardsley, *Caprice. Verso: Masked Woman with a White Mouse, c.* 1894, oil on canvas.

Gustav Klimt,
Fable, 1883,
oil on canvas.

waistcoat as he kisses them and calls them by all sorts of endear-
ing names. White mice resonate with female sexuality and
imaginings of the phallus in Gustav Klimt's *Fable* and Aubrey
Beardsley's *Caprice. Verso: Masked Woman with a White Mouse*.
White mice rarely feature in works of art much before this
period, since this rare variety had not yet appeared in fancying.

As art turned from exploring physical reality to the human
mind in the eighteenth century, the mouse – covert, wild and at

the level of the earth – had become a particularly useful animal for thinking about the hidden, darker and more uncontrollable of human emotions: the base desires concealed beneath (quite literally in Aubrey Beardsley's piece) the 'mask' of civilization.

Even in children's fairy tales, which became a popular source for artistic inspiration during the Romantic period, the seemingly innocent, anthropomorphic, magical and avenging mouse retains its sexual connotations. Bruno Bettelheim discusses in his psychological analyses of fairy tales how mice embody the 'dirty' thoughts of the child. When mice become modes of transport for children in book traditions, examples of which we see from the eighteenth and nineteenth centuries, apart from the fact that mouse vehicles befit the human characters' small frames, they more importantly function as physical extensions of their riders' sexual selves: of growing fertility and the impurity of puberty. Tom Thumb, for example, a symbol of the growing phallus, is pictured riding in a chariot pulled by mice; and Alice, a young girl who experiences surreal changes in her bodily form after falling down a symbolic hole in *Alice's Adventures in*

John Tenniel's depiction of Alice and a mouse in the Pool of Tears from Lewis Carroll's *Alice's Adventures in Wonderland* (1891).

Wonderland, finds herself traversing the purifying waters of the Pool of Tears on the back of a mouse.

With the medical progress of the eighteenth and nineteenth centuries, the mouse also became significant to children as a symbol of the penetrative nature of disease as well as the phallus; its trap a symbol of protection and accomplishment. Women, as guardians of fertility, are pictured with children in late nineteenth-century paintings triumphantly holding mice, symbols of death, ensnared in cages.

A less positive picture is painted in E.T.A. Hoffmann's children's story 'The Nutcracker and the Mouse King' (1816), in which a seven-headed mouse appears as a disease demon which

John Constable, *Mouse with a Piece of Cheese*, 1824, drawing on paper.

tries to possess the heroine (who we imagine to represent the author's daughter, who died of cholera). The story describes the sovereign mouse 'emanating from the floorboards', as if by some 'subterranean force', his seven 'hissing' heads 'adorned with seven diadems' (an image seemingly drawn from the old Serpent of Rome in the Bible, a beast who shares the same number of heads, 'wears seven crowns, and is called the devil': Revelations 12:3, 9). The number seven is significant in that it references the seven demons that possessed Mary Magdalene, while the 'oozing of blood red foam' from all seven of the rodent's mouths is perhaps an allusion to the symptom of the disease. This is a very rare example of a villainous mouse in children's fiction. This particular story continues to be performed by the English National Ballet, having been adapted in the late nineteenth century with music composed by Tchaikovsky. (Usually, probably for ease of movement, the Mouse King is only given one head.)

A popular illustration of a motherly mouse by Beatrix Potter in *The Tale of Two Bad Mice*.

The mouse's evolution in visual culture was marked by the birth of Mickey Mouse a century or so later in the late 1920s; a 'mouse' that metaphorically, physically and technologically reasserted the rodent as an animal of modernity. True to the mouse's modern mission, the icon of Mickey embodied the new kitsch aesthetic of popular culture, which was both praised and criticized for its relationship to new technologies that were viewed as liberating and homogenizing, progressive and degenerative. The famous mouse was likened to the productions of the Dada movement, which was characterized by its use of photomontage and was accused by critical thinkers, such as Theodor Adorno (1903–1969) of the Frankfurt School of social theory, of creating a manufactured experience and representing mechanically produced culture.[6]

Disney's early illustrations of Mickey show a gradual process of 'demousification', resulting in a character who stood upright; his feet, the telltale signs of animality, covered; his defining tail only hinted at, his whiskers barely visible and his face more like that of a dog than a mouse. Mickey was really the first 'post-modern animal'. His stylized, nonmouse-like design seems to be a reinterpretation of modernist experimental genres that challenged conventional ideas about art and reality. A Dada embossed pencil drawing by Californian artist Ben Berlin, entitled *Portrait* (1923), is an example of works of the period that, through their lines and abstract shapes, resonate with Mickey's distorted form. To some extent Mickey Mouse expressed the Surrealist mood, embodying, as one art critic put it in a review of an exhibition by the artist Max Ernst, 'a world of dreams where almost anything is liable to happen'.[7] The Surrealist movement became popular in the early days of Hollywood, per-haps slightly later than the creation of Mickey Mouse. Still, its major theme of self-portraiture, referencing the artist's encounter

Ben Berlin,
Portrait, 1923,
pencil with
embossing.

between interior and exterior worlds, seems to reflect Disney's creation of Mickey – whom Disney voiced himself – as a realization of his own alter ego . It is suggested that Mickey embodies the filmmaker's feeling of being an 'eternal outsider'.[8]

Many commentators of Disney suggest that it was Disney's feeling of not belonging that inspired the immigrant identity of Mickey, who fused African-American and Jewish racist stereotypes. The mouse, as vermin and as a symbol of the underclass, is an animal best suited to representations of 'inferiority'. In fairy tales he is the ultimate rags-to-riches type, and was therefore perfect for conveying social mobility and equality as part of the American Dream. Mickey Mouse's colour-block face and white gloves are accepted as a reference to 'blackface'. One author on the subject of Mickey Mouse draws a comparison between Mickey's defining snout and Patricia Erens's theory that Jewish ethnicity was identified in early cinema by the characters being played by actors with large noses.[9] Some commentators have suggested that the depiction of Mickey Mouse as a figure of pro-Jewish propaganda, as a 'charming, clean do-gooder',[10] served as a political response to Hitler's anti-Semitic campaign, which, channelled though films, posters and other visual media,

Mickey Mouse
film still, 1931.

A giant Mickey Mouse in Macy's Thanksgiving Day Parade of 1934, making mice of the people at his feet.

compared Jews to vermin, painting them as 'dirty'. (American cartoonist Art Spiegelman much later drew more explicitly on the same metaphor in his graphic novel *Maus* of 1986 and 1991, which illustrated his father's survival of the Holocaust.) Mickey's image was seen as both neoconservative and anti-fascist. On the one hand the Nazis considered Mickey Mouse a grotesque insult to high culture and an example of pro-Jewish propaganda;

on the other they used his image, perhaps mockingly, on 'everything from bomber planes to coffee cups'.[11]

Following the success of Mickey Mouse, other mouse characters became popular in children's entertainment: in comics of the 1940s such as *Mighty Mouse*, which parodied Superman, and, on television in the same decade, in Hanna-Barbera's famous animated cat and mouse series *Tom & Jerry*.

After the Second World War, Mickey Mouse, like other 'trashy' everyday American exports, represented exciting, new-found consumption. Postwar artists such as Eduardo Paolozzi

Liliana Porter,
Dialogue with Christ/Lamp, 1999,
collage on paper.

and Roy Lichtenstein drew upon Mickey Mouse and other cartoon characters, positioned alongside commercial imagery, in Pop art or 'neo-Dada' renderings of 'pre-packaged modernities'. Paolozzi even started to use images of real mice as metaphors for Mickey. In 1970 he produced an etching, laid out as if in comic book panels, entitled *Pages from the Aerospace Medical Library: Geometry Relations in Electron Irradiation of a Mouse, 11:47pm, 11:53pm, 12:06am*. In it, three x-rays of real laboratory mice at different aspects are displayed above repeated images of Coca-Cola bottles, suggesting the modern ephemerality of life and consumption, technology and mass production, and the aesthetic parallel between the real and the artificial.

Mickey's oversized ears quickly became globally accepted as a sign for 'mouseness', which goes to show how comfortable we became with the mutated, hyperreal image of the rodent. In the 1970s Pop art sculptor Claes Oldenburg produced a sculpture of an angular silhouette of Mickey Mouse's head, simply entitled *Geometric Mouse* (1971). It sits with other examples in which an allusion to Mickey's Mouse (the 'hyperreal hyperreal'), solely referred to as 'mouse', becomes a sort of pattern or prototype for mass production, as in the technical lithograph *System of Iconography: Plug Mouse, Good Humour, Lipstick, Switches* (1970–71).

Despite Mickey's all-pervasive image, British television featured other popular mouse characters in puppet shows of the 1960s and '70s, such as the Italian foam-mouse Topo Gigio and the BBC's knitted Clangers of the early 1970s, which were handmade and operated by humans rather than machines.

In the 1990s the Argentinian-born artist Liliana Porter connected Mickey Mouse to the mass-produced postmodern image of Che Guevara's face. (It seems that Mickey Mouse can be substituted for anything or anyone as an overriding reference to the power of postmodern consumer culture, even blasphemously appearing in an online image as Christ at the Last Supper.) In one digital print Porter superimposes the images of the rodent and Che Guevara on top of a page from a nineteenth-century poetic novel, *The Songs of Maldoror*, which inspired a number of early Surrealist artists. The print, entitled *Maldoror* (1994), is named after the book's misanthropic protagonist, implying an evil rather than an emancipatory nature in the two famous icons. In another piece, *Dialogue with Christ/Lamp* (1999), Mickey appears to be justifying himself to a kitsch rendering of Christ. Perhaps a society that is becoming increasingly concerned about sustainability is becoming tired of images that perpetuate a throwaway culture, particularly those that demand exaltation.

Like the real mouse, Mickey is an infinite paradox that can be interpreted in many ways. Like the real mouse, we can talk about him as a symbol of globalization, 'colonizing' the world or 'infesting' and 'threatening' indigenous cultures, his image constantly 'reproducing' in the work of others from model-makers to fashion designers. (In recent years Comme des Garçons, Manish Arora and Jeremy Scott have all presented the image of Mickey or Minnie Mouse in their shows.)

Impressions of 'real mice' continue to connote the changing human world in the twenty-first century. We have already seen artists such as Patricia Piccinini and Lynn Randolph make the laboratory mouse, depicted as a sort of post-human/animal figure, their subject. It is very likely that we will see the laboratory mouse appear in examples of bio-art in the twenty-first century. Another contemporary American artist, Tiffany Bozic, deals with the theme of creation in her untitled spherical installation of incredibly realistic painted mice hanging in goose eggs (2006). This, like many other depictions of mice en masse in repeated shapes forming single-cell-like structures, appears to allude to

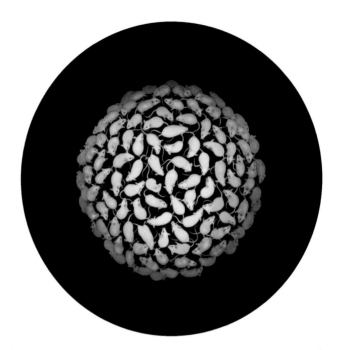

Tiffany Bozic, 'Mouseball', 2006, acrylic on maple panel.

unending digital space, nanotechnology and cloning. David Falconer's *Vermin Death Stack* (1998), an upwards-pointing tornado of dead mice and rats at the Saatchi Gallery, and fashion designer Charlie Le Mindu's rodent-carcass headdress from London Fashion Week in 2009 seem to speak of equality, excess, mass production, monotony or control in modern society.

The mouse has always played a powerful role in Western culture. It does not appear in art for art's sake: as decoration or as a prop in impressions of human life, used to provide a sense of time or place. Discreet or brazen, real or mythic, the presence of the mouse always conveys an important message. These messages are not necessarily grand or divine in their sentiments, but instead are very real, and of the moment; reminding us of

134

Mechanical mouse automaton, gold with pearls, life-size, attributed to Henri Maillardet, *c.* 1810.

the true nature of our society, of our psyche and our mortality. The mouse is used to think about possible futures, both positive and negative. This suggests that somehow we identify with the mouse much more than we think; perhaps more than with any other animal. Maybe this is because the mouse, in its multifarious ways, represents what we do to the universe.

Timeline of the Mouse

250–200 MYA	200–145.5 MYA	142–65 MYA	54.8–33.7 MYA	33.7–23.8 MYA
(Triassic) *Megazostrodon*, the earliest shrew-like mammals appear	(Jurassic) Evolution of the Multituberculata, or 'Rodents of the Mesozoic'	(Cretaceous) 'Rodents' thrive under the emergence and radiation of flowering plants	(Eocene) Multituberculata replaced by 'true rodents'. Appearance of the oldest known rodent, *Ischyromys* (early Eocene)	(Oligocene) Over half of all living rodent families have appeared

2600 BC	1700 BC	1100 BC	AD 1775
The mouse is depicted in paintings of the first recorded 'dentist', the ancient Egyptian Hesi-Re	Some of the oldest records of mouse infestations, in houses in Petrie, Egypt	Earliest record of mouse breeding from the Chinese encyclopaedia the *Erya*, which notes 'dancing mice', 'yellow mice' and mice with 'dominant spotting'	Perhaps the earliest text on mouse breeding is produced in Japan, *Yoso-tama-no-kakehashi* or 'a bridge to obtaining novel jewel-like *nezumi*'

1905	1928	1929	V1935
Harvard begins working with tumours in Japanese waltzing mice, concluding that cancer has a genetic basis Pink-eye mouse variety introduced to mouse fancying	Mickey Mouse makes his debut in *Steamboat Willie*	Charles C. Little founds the Jackson Laboratory	*An Eighteenth Century Japanese Guide-book on Mouse Breeding* is introduced to the Western scientific community

23.8–2.6 MYA	13.75 MYA	11,700 BC	C. 7500 BC–5700 BC
(Miocene/Pliocene) Appearance of Dipodidae jumping mice in Old and New World's emergence of true ancestor of Muridae	(Miocene) Approximate date given to the earliest molars currently accepted as murine, discovered in Siwalik Hills, Pakistan	(Beginning of Holocene) Muridae are by now common around the world as glaciers retreat and humans migrate	Earliest suggestions of mouse worship/ association with the goddess, from the burial of an important woman with a necklace of mouse bones in the Neolithic settlement of Çatal Hüyük in Anatolia

1787	1859	1892	1895
Kyoto money exchanger Chobei Zenya produces a booklet on the 'breeding of curious varieties of the mouse', *Chinganso-date-gusa*	Charles Darwin's *On the Origin of Species* is published	Fancy mice are first shown at a small livestock exhibition in Oxford	Mr Walter Maxey, 'the Father of the Fancy', founds the National Mouse Club

1941	1980	1990	1999	2006
The Jackson Laboratory publishes the first textbook on the lab mouse, *Biology of Laboratory Mouse*, almost half of which is dedicated to cancer biology	Decade sees the birth of the first patented animal, OncoMouse, genetically engin- eered for breast cancer research	Decade sees 'Humanized Mice' engineered to have human genes, cells, tissues and/or organs	Murphy Roth Large (MRL) mouse is discovered in 1999 to possess incredible regenerative capa- bilities unnatural to other mammals	Scientists find a mouse with a natural resistance to cancer, which they call 'Super Mouse'

References

INTRODUCTION: *RIDICULUS MUS*

1 St Isidore (of Seville), *Etymologies*, trans. Stephen A. Barney
  (Cambridge, 2006), p. 254.
2 John G. Wood, *Bible Animals* (London, 1869), p. 94.
3 E.B.N. Dhabhar, *Persian Sad-dar*, p. 34, quoted in Jivanji J. Modi,
  'The Rat Problem and the Ancients' [1902], in Modi,
  Anthropological Papers (Bombay, 1911), pp. 355–65.
4 Horace, *The Satires and Epistles of Horace*, trans. Smith Palmer
  Bovie (Chicago, IL, 2002), p. 92.

1 THE EVOLUTION OF THE MOUSE

1 J. Pelikan, 'Patterns of Reproduction in the House Mouse', in
  *Biology of the House Mouse: Symposia of the Zoological Society of
  London*, No. 47, ed. R. J. Berry (London, 1981), p. 205.
2 Jason A. Lillegraven, Zofia Kielan-Jaworowska and William A.
  Clemens, eds, *Mesozoic Mammals: The First Two-thirds of
  Mammalian History* (Berkeley, CA, 1979), p. 99.
3 Terry A. Vaughn, James M. Ryan and Nicholas J. Czaplewski,
  Mammology (London, 2010), p. 200.
4 Ibid.
5 Ronald M. Nowak, *Walker's Mammals of the World* (Baltimore,
  MD, 1999), vol. II, p. 1517.
6 Charles F. Partington, *The British Cyclopaedia of Natural History*
  (London, 1837), p. 526.

7 Don E. Wilson and DeeAnn M. Reeder, *Mammal Species of the World: A Taxonomic and Geographic Reference* (Baltimore, MD, 2005), vol. XII, p. 751.

8 Bill Breed and Fred Ford, *Native Mice and Rats* (Collingwood, Victoria, 2007), p. 2.

9 Donald Brothwell, 'The Pleistocene and Holocene Archaeology of the House Mouse and Related Species', in *Biology of the House Mouse*, ed. Berry, p. 10.

10 Wilson and Reeder, *Mammal Species of the World*, vol. XII, p. 1389.

11 Brothwell, 'The Pleistocene and Holocene Archaeology of the House Mouse and Related Species', p. 1.

12 Francesco Di Castri, A. J. Hansen and M. Debussche, *Biological Invasions in Europe and the Mediterranean Basin* (Alphen aan den Rijn, 1990), p. 278.

13 Brothwell, 'The Pleistocene and Holocene Archaeology of the House Mouse and Related Species', p. 1.

14 J. G. Fox, *The Mouse in Biomedical Research* (London, 2007), p. 29.

15 Daniel Simberloff and Marcel Rejmánek, *Encyclopedia of Biological Invasions* (Los Angeles, CA, 2011), p. 120.

16 T. Kuramoto, 'Yoso-tama-no-kakehashi: The First Japanese Guidebook on Raising Rats', in *Experimental Animals*, LX/I (2011), pp. 1–6.

17 Ibid.

19 William F. Edwards, *Des Caractères Physiologiques des Races Humaines* (Paris, 1829), pp. 25–6; John S. Gaskoin, 'On a Peculiar Variety of *Mus musculus*', *Proceedings of the Zoological Society of London* (London, 1856), p. 40.

20 Ibid.

21 George Forrest, *Every Boy's Book* (London, 1855), p. 309.

22 John Davidson Goodman, *American Natural History* (Philadelphia, PA, 1831), p. 85.

23 Anonymous, 'Biography of the Mouse', *Irish Penny Journal*, I (1840–41), p. 221.

24 Mark Jason, *The Oxford Handbook of the History of Medicine* (Oxford, 2011), p. 570.

25 Karen Ann Rader, *Making Mice: Standardizing Animals for American Biomedical Research, 1900–1955* (Oxford, 2004), p. 32.

26 'Scientists in a Shoebox', BBC Radio 4, 4 and 11 February 2004.

27 'It's a Miracle – Mice Regrow Hearts', http://worldhealth.net (16 September 2005) (accessed April 2009).

2 THE MOUSE IN EGYPT, GREECE AND ROME

1 Donald Brothwell, 'The Pleistocene and Holocene Archaeology of the House Mouse and Related Species', in *Biology of the House Mouse: Symposia of the Zoological Society of London,* no. 47, ed. R. J. Berry (London, 1981), p. 1.

2 Ibid.

3 Strabo, *The Geography of Strabo*, trans. H. C. Hamilton Esq. and W. Falcone (London, 1856), vol. XIII, p. 373; Aelian, *On the Characteristics of Animals*, trans. Alwyn Faber Scholfield (Cambridge, MA, 1972), p. 15; Pliny the Elder, *Natural History in Thirty-Seven Books*, trans. Philemon Holland (London, 1847–8), vol. I, p. 59; Anne Burton, *Diodorus Siculus: A Commentary* (Leiden, 1972), Book I, p. 53.

4 Theophrastus reported in Pliny, *Natural History*, Books VIII–XI, p. 222.

5 Aristotle, *A History of Animals in Ten Books*, trans. Richard Creswell (London, 1878), p. 178.

6 F. S. Bodenheimer, *Animal and Man in Bible Lands* (Leiden, 1960), p. 47.

7 Andrew Lang, *Custom and Myth* (New York, 2007), p. 111.

8 Ibid., p. 113.

9 St Isidore (of Seville), *Etymologies*, trans. Stephen A. Barney (Cambridge, 2006), p. 254.

10 Pliny, *Natural History*, Book XI, quoted in Warren R. Dawson, *The Bridle of Pegasus* (Whitefish, MT, 2003), p. 110.

11 W. J. Loftie, *An Essay on Scarabs* (London, 1884), pp. xxiv–xxv.

12 Dawson, *Bridle of Pegasus*, p. 104

13 Harold Bayley, *The Lost Language of Symbolism* (New York, 2006), p. 300.

14 Charles J. S. Thompson, *Alchemy: Source of Chemistry and Medicine* (Whitefish, MT, 2003) p. 172.

15 Immanuel Velikovsky, *Worlds in Collision* (New York, 2009), p. 233.

16 Lang, *Custom and Myth*, p. 117.

17 Aristotle, *The Rhetoric of Aristotle*, trans. J. E. Sandy (London, 1909), p. 132.

18 R. W. Sharples, P. M. Huby and W. W. Fortenbaugh, *Theophrastus of Eresus: Sources on Biology* (Leiden, 1995), p. 66.

19 See Nikolay P. Grinster, 'What Did Mysteries Mean to the Ancient Greeks?' (2008), at http//:scholar.lib.vt.edu (accessed April 2010).

20 Ibid.

21 Ibid.

22 Margaret Alexiou, *After Antiquity: Greek Language, Myth, and Metaphor* (New York, 2002), p. 108.

23 Ibid., p. 108.

24 Aristotle, *A History of Animals in Ten Books*, p. 178.

25 Ibid.

26 Ibid.

27 Desiderius Erasmus and Margaret Mann Phillips, trans., *Adages* (Toronto, n.d.), vol. XXXIV.

28 See Lang, *Custom and Myth*, pp. 103–21.

29 See Marion Roalfe Cox, *Cinderella: 345 Variants* (London, 1895).

30 Harold Bayley, *The Lost Language of Symbolism* (New York, 2006), p. 192.

31 Ibid., p. 255.

32 Ibid., p. 46.

33 *Collections from the Greek Anthology* (London, 1813), p. 475.

34 Andrew Dalby, *Food in the Ancient World From A–Z* (London, 2003), p. 257.

35 Pliny, *Natural History*, trans. and ed. J. Bostock and H. T. Riley (London, 1857), vol. V, p. 416.

36 Ibid.
37 Pliny, *Natural History*, trans. Bostock and Riley, vol. v, p. 448.
38 Charles G. Leland, *Arcadia: The Gospel of Witches* (New York, 1968), p. 24.

3 THE ASIAN MOUSE

1 Alexandra A. E. Van de Geer, *Animals in Stone: Indian Animals Sculpted Through Time* (Leiden, 2008), p. 78.
2 James G. Fox, *The Mouse in Biomedical Research* (London, 2007), p. 29.
3 Muhammad S. Adbul-Rahman, *The Meaning and Exploration of the Glorious Qur'an*, 2nd edn (London, 2009), vol. III, p. 28.
4 *Mbh.* XV, 34, 18; Dr Trilok C. Majupuria, *Sacred and Symbolic Animals of Nepal* (Kathmandu, 1977), p. 141.
5 Debiprasad Cahttopadhyaya, *Studies in the History of Indian Philosophy* (Calcutta, 1980), p. 218.
6 Om Prakash Joshi, *Gods of Heaven, Home of Gods: Studies of Popular Prints* (Jaipur, 1939), p. 73.
7 Robert L. Brown, *Ganesh: Studies of an Asian God* (New York, 1991), p. 19.
8 Andrew Lang, *Custom and Myth* (New York, 2007), p. 116.
9 Alain Daniélou, *The Myths and Gods of India* (New York, 1991), p. 296.
10 Asis Sen, *Animal Motifs in Ancient Indian Art* (Calcutta, 1969), p. 26.
11 W. F. O'Connor, *Folk Tales from Tibet* (Whitefish, MT, 2004), p. 74.
12 Majupuria, *Sacred and Symbolic Animals of Nepal*, p. 140.
13 Alain Daniélou, *Hindu Polytheism* (London, 1964), p. 297.
14 John A. Grimes, *Ganapati: Song of the Self* (New York, 1995), p. 86.
15 James G. Frazer, *The Golden Bough: A Study in Magic and Religion* (London, 1922), p. 540.
16 Hope B. Werness, *The Continuum Encyclopaedia of Animal Symbolism in Art* (London, 2006), p. 285.

17 T. Kuramoto, 'Yoso-tama-no-kakehashi: The First Japanese Guidebook on Raising Rats', in *Experimental Animals*, LX/1 (2011), pp. 1–6.

4 THE MOUSE IN THE INDIGENOUS CULTURES OF THE AMERICAS

1 Bernadino de Sahagún, *General History of the Things of New Spain: Florentine Codex. Book II: Earthly Things, translated from the Aztec into English, with Notes and Illustrations* (Salt Lake City, UT, 1963), p. 17.

2 Victoria Schlesinger, *Animals and Plants of the Ancient Maya: A Guide* (Austin, TX, 1999), p. 83.

3 John F. Eisenberg and Kent H. Redford, *Mammals of the Neotropics*, vol. III: *Ecuador, Bolivia, Brazil* (Chicago, IL, 1999), p. 16.

4 Carl Lumholtz, *Unknown Mexico: A Record of Five Years' Exploration Among the Tribes of the Western Sierra Madre* (Cambridge, 2011), vol. II, p. 262.

5 Hope B. Werness, *The Continuum Encyclopaedia of Animal Symbolism in Art* (London, 2006), p. 48.

6 Gabrielle Vail, Anthony F. Aveni, *The Madrid Codex: New Approaches to Understanding an Ancient Mayan Manuscript* (Denver, CO, 2004), p. 327.

7 Manuel Aguilar-Moreno, *Handbook to Life in the Aztec World* (Oxford, 2007), p. 304.

8 *Estudios de cultura Náhuatl* (Mexico City, 1984), vol. XVII, p. 102.

9 Martín de la Cruz, *An Aztec Herbal: The Classic Codex of 1552* (Baltimore, MD, 1939), p. 94.

10 Miguel de Asúa and Roger Kenneth French, *A New World of Animals: Early Modern Europeans on the Creatures of Iberian America* (Aldershot, Hants, 2005), p. 45.

11 David Carrasco and Scott Sessions, *Cave, City, and Eagle's Nest: An Interpretive Journey through the Mapa de Cuauhtinchan*, issue 2 (Albuquerque, NM, 2007), p. 211.

12 Alfred W. Bowers, *Hidatsa Social and Ceremonial Organization* (Lincoln, NE, 1992), p. 134.

13 Barry Pritzker, *A Native American Encyclopaedia: History, Culture and Peoples* (Oxford, 2000), p. 118.

14 George Thornton Emmons, *The Tlingit Indians* (Washington, DC, 1991), p. 399.

15 Ibid.

16 See Ethel G. Stewart, *The Dene and Na-Dene Indian Migration – 1233 AD: Escape from Genghis Khan* (Chicago, IL, 1991), and Gloria Farley, 'Mouse God with a Pointed Snout', at www.midwesternepigraphic.org.

17 See Nikolay P. Grinster, 'What Did Mysteries Mean to the Ancient Greeks?' (2008), at http://scholar.lib.vt.edu, accessed April 2010).

18 Emmons, *The Tlingit Indians*, p. 163.

19 Franz Boas, *Eskimo of Baffin Island*, quoted in Waldemar Bogoras, 'The Folklore of Northeastern Asia, as Compared with that of Northwestern Americas', *American Anthropologist*, IV/4 (October–December 1902), pp. 577–683.

5 THE MOUSE IN ART, FILM AND LITERATURE

1 Herbert Friedmann, *Bestiary for Saint Jerome* (Washington, DC, 1980), p. 271.

2 Erwin Panofsky, *Studies in Iconology*, quoted ibid., p. 271.

3 Richard Barber, *Bestiary: Being an English Version of the Bodleian Library* (Oxford, 2006), p. 109.

4 Otto Neustratter, 'Mice in Plague Pictures', *Journal of Walter's Art Gallery*, 4 (1941), pp. 105–14.

5 John C. Cavadini, *Augustine through the Ages: An Encyclopaedia* (Cambridge, 1999), p. 704.

6 Miriam Bratu Hansen, *Cinema and Experience: Siegfried Kracauer, Walter Benjamin, and Theodor W. Adorno* (Berkeley, CA, 2012), p. 169.

7 Susan M. Anderson, 'Journey into the Sun: Californian Artists and Surrealism', in *On the Edge of America: California Modernist Art, 1900–1950*, ed. Paul J. Karlstrom (Berkeley, CA, 1996).

8 Douglas Brode, *Multiculturalism and the Mouse: Race and Sex in Disney Entertainment* (Austin, TX, 2005), p. 105.

9 Ibid.

10 Ibid., p. 106.

11 Carsten Laqua, *Wie Mickey unter die Nazis fiel: Walt Disney und Deutschland* (Berlin, 1992), pp. 104–5, 108, quoted in Richard Burt, *The Administration of Aesthetics: Censorship, Political Criticism, and the Public Sphere* (Minneapolis, MN, 1994), p. 248.

Select Bibliography

Aristotle, *A History of Animals in Ten Books*, trans. Richard Cresswell
    (London, 1878)
Armstrong, Philip, *What Animals Mean in the Fiction of Modernity*
    (Oxford, 2008)
Baker, Steve, *Picturing the Beast* (Manchester, 1993)
Ball, Katherine M., *Animal Motifs in Asian Art: An Illustrated Guide to
    their Meanings and Aesthetics* (New York, 2004)
Bayley, Harold, *The Lost Language of Symbolism* (New York, 2006)
Bell, Elizabeth, Lynda Haas and Laura Sells, eds, *From Mouse to
    Mermaid: The Politics of Film, Gender, and Culture* (Bloomington,
    IN, 1995)
Berry, R. J., ed., *Biology of the House Mouse*: *Symposia of the Zoological
    Society of London*, 47 (London, 1981)
Cirlot, Juan E., *A Dictionary of Symbols* (New York, 1972)
Dawson, Warren R., *Bridle of Pegasus* (Whitefish, MT, 2003)
Douglas, Mary, *Purity and Danger: An Analysis of Concepts of Pollution
    and Taboo* (Oxford, 2002)
Fox, James G., *The Mouse in Biomedical Research* (London, 2007)
Frazer, James G., *The Golden Bough: A Study in Magic and Religion*
    (New York, 1947)
Friedmann, Herbert, *Bestiary of St Jerome* (Washington, DC, 1980)
Grimm, Jacob, and James S. Stallybrass, *Teutonic Mythology* (New
    York, 2004), vol. III
Haraway, Donna, *Modest-Witness@Second_Millenium.FemaleMan_
    Meets_OncoMouse* (New York, 1997)

—, *The Haraway Reader* (New York, 2004)

Harris, James R., *The Ascent of Olympus* (London, 1917)

Hedrich, Hans J., and Gillian R. Bullock, *The Laboratory Mouse* (London, 2004)

Hinton, M.A.C., *Rats and Mice as Enemies of Mankind* (New York, 2008)

Homer, *The Hymns of Homer*, trans. George Chapman and Samuel W. Singer (London, 1818)

Isidore (St, of Seville), *Etymologies*, trans. Stephen A. Barney (Cambridge, 2006)

Lang, Andrew, *Custom and Myth* (New York, 2007)

Lévi-Strauss, Claude, *The Savage Mind* (London, 1966)

MacKenzie, Donald A., *Myths of Babylonia and Assyria* (New York, 2007)

—, and A. Moncrieff, *Myths of Crete and Pre-Hellenic Europe* (New York, 2010)

Massey, Gerald, *Ancient Egypt: The Light of the World* (New York, 2007)

Pliny, *Natural History*, trans. H. Rackham (Cambridge, MA, 1938–40), Books I–XI

Rader, Karen, *Making Mice: Standardizing Animals for American Biomedical Research, 1900–1955* (Princeton, NJ, 2004)

Thorndike, Lynn, *History of Magic and Experimental Science* (London, 1967)

Topsell, Edward, *The Historie of Foure-footed Beastes* (London, 1607)

Vaughn, Terry A., James M. Ryan and Nicholas J. Czaplewski, *Mammology* (London, 2010)

Werness, Hope B., *The Continuum Encyclopaedia of Animal Symbolism in Art* (London, 2006)

Wood, John G., *Bible Animals* (London, 1869)

Associations and Websites

Websites about mice, or those that include information on them, are often related to the animal's control, listing the rodent (particularly but not exclusively the house mouse) among other so-called pests in need of extermination. There are, however, some online resources for the care and protection of and education about mice, listed below, together with established associations for the breeding of fancy mice.

THE AMERICAN FANCY RAT AND MOUSE ASSOCIATION
www.afrma.org
Founded in 1983, this is a non-profit international club. Anyone that has an interest in rats or mice can be a member. AFRMA promotes and encourages breeding and exhibiting, educating the public on the animals' positive qualities as companions, and providing information on their proper care. Competition shows are held several times a year in southern California.

BBC WILDLIFE
www.bbc.co.uk/nature/life/muridae
This site includes clear and informative facts about Old World mice and rats, with links to pages dedicated to their New World cousins, and to other rodential species.

LONDON AND SOUTHERN COUNTIES MOUSE AND RAT CLUB
www.miceandrats.com
Founded in 1916, this is a club for owners, breeders and exhibitors of fancy mice and rats.

NATIONAL MOUSE CLUB
www.thenationalmouseclub.co.uk
Formed over a century ago, the NMC encourages the breeding and exhibiting of fancy mice, publishes the rules and standards by which mice are judged, and gives support to shows throughout the UK.

NATURAL ENGLAND
www.naturalengland.org.uk/ourwork/regulation/wildlife/species/
    hazeldormice.aspx
Provides advice, licensing and legislation relating to the hazel dormouse.

PEOPLE FOR THE ETHICAL TREATMENT OF ANIMALS
www.peta.org/issues/wildlife/living-harmony-wildlife/house-mice
PETA puts an excellent case for the positive qualities in mice and rats, explaining how we can live in harmony with what society deems 'vermin'.

THE WILDLIFE TRUST
www.wildlifetrusts.org/how-you-can-help/adopt-species/
    adopt-dormouse
Allows those concerned to adopt a dormouse, water vole or any one of a variety of other British mammals, in a number of counties across the UK.

Acknowledgements

I would like to give thanks to the libraries of the Zoological Society of London, the Department of Egypt and Sudan at the British Museum, the Special Collections Library at the University of Maine and the Tobey C. Moss Gallery, Los Angeles, as well as to artists Tiffany Bozic, Patricia Piccinini, Lynn Randolph and Jay Simeon (by way of the Douglas Reynolds Gallery, Vancouver) for allowing me to use pieces of their wonderful work in this book. A special thank you also to the great friends and family who have supported the writing of this book at every turn, and feigned most kindly and brilliantly an interest in my relentless discussion about rodents.

Thank you so much.

Photo Acknowledgements

The author and publishers wish to express their thanks to the below sources of illustrative material and/or permission to reproduce it. Some locations of artworks are also given below.

From John James Audubon and John Bachman, *Viviparous Quadrupeds of North America* (New York, 1845–54): p. 96; The Bowes Museum, Barnard Castle, Co. Durham: p. 135; courtesy of the artist (Tiffany Bozic): p. 134; British Library, London (photo © The British Library Board): p. 66; The British Museum, London (photos © Trustees of the British Museum): pp. 79, 80, 125; photos © Trustees of the British Museum, London: pp. 46, 108, 119, 121; Brooklyn Museum, New York: pp. 8, 12; photo Brooklyn Museum, New York: p. 87; from Lewis Carroll, *Alice's Adventures in Wonderland*: pp. 31 (London, 1865), 124 (London, 1891); courtesy of the Douglas Reynolds Gallery, Vancouver: p. 95; Egyptian Museum, Cairo: p. 48; from *Les Fables de La Fontaine illustrées par Gustave Doré* (Paris, 1868): p. 54; Galleria degli Uffizi, Florence (image courtesy of Scala Archives, Florence – courtesy of the Ministero per i Beni e le Attività Culturali): p. 117; Galleria Nazionale, Rome: p. 118; from John Gaskoin, 'On a Peculiar Variety of *Mus musculus*', in *Proceedings of the Zoological Society of London*, Part XXIV (1856): p. 30; Historisches Museum, Vienna: p. 123; from Georges Louis Leclerc, Comte de Buffon, *Compléments du Buffon: Races Humains et Mammifères* (Paris, 1838): p. 16; from Heinrich Lichtenstein, *Darstellung neuer oder wenig bekannter Säugethiere . . .* (Berlin, 1827–34): p. 43; photo 'Lord Mountbatten': p. 44; Los Angeles County Museum

Under the following conditions:

attribution – readers must attribute any image in the manner specified by the author or licensor (but not in any way that suggests that these parties endorse them or their use of the work).

Index